HOLT SCIENCE & TECHNOLOGY

Weather and Climate

HOLT, RINEHART AND WINSTON

A Harcourt Classroom Education Company

Austin • **New York** • **Orlando** • **Atlanta** • **San Francisco** • **Boston** • **Dallas** • **Toronto** • **London**

Staff Credits

Editorial

Robert W. Todd, Executive Editor

Robert V. Tucek, Leigh Ann Garcia, Senior Editors

Clay Walton, Jim Ratcliffe, Editors

ANCILLARIES

Jennifer Childers, Senior Editor

Chris Colby, Molly Frohlich, Shari Husain, Kristen McCardel, Sabelyn Pussman, Erin Roberson

COPYEDITING

Dawn Spinozza, Copyediting Supervisor

EDITORIAL SUPPORT STAFF

Jeanne Graham, Mary Helbling, Tanu'e White, Doug Rutley

EDITORIAL PERMISSIONS

Cathy Paré, Permissions Manager

Jan Harrington, Permissions Editor

Art, Design, and Photo

BOOK DESIGN

Richard Metzger, Design Director

Marc Cooper, Senior Designer

José Garza, Designer

Alicia Sullivan, Designer (ATE), Cristina Bowerman, Design Associate (ATE), Eric Rupprath, Designer (Ancillaries), Holly Whittaker, Traffic Coordinator

IMAGE ACQUISITIONS

Joe London, Director

Elaine Tate, Art Buyer Supervisor

Jeannie Taylor, Photo Research Supervisor

Andy Christiansen, Photo Researcher

Jackie Berger, Assistant Photo Researcher

PHOTO STUDIO

Sam Dudgeon, Senior Staff Photographer

Victoria Smith, Photo Specialist

Lauren Eischen, Photo Coordinator

DESIGN NEW MEDIA

Susan Michael, Design Director

Production

Mimi Stockdell, Senior Production Manager

Beth Sample, Senior Production Coordinator

Suzanne Brooks, Sara Carroll-Downs

Media Production

Kim A. Scott, Senior Production Manager

Adriana Bardin-Prestwood, Senior Production Coordinator

New Media

Armin Gutzmer, Director

Jim Bruno, Senior Project Manager

Lydia Doty, Senior Project Manager

Jessica Bega, Project Manager

Cathy Kuhles, Nina Degollado, Technical Assistants

Design Implementation and Production

The Quarasan Group, Inc.

Acknowledgments

Chapter Writers

Kathleen Meehan Berry
Science Chairman
Canon-McMillan School District
Canonsburg, Pennsylvania

Robert H. Fronk, Ph.D.
Chair of Science and Mathematics Education Department
Florida Institute of Technology
West Melbourne, Florida

Mary Kay Hemenway, Ph.D.
Research Associate and Senior Lecturer
Department of Astronomy
The University of Texas
Austin, Texas

Kathleen Kaska
Life and Earth Science Teacher
Lake Travis Middle School
Austin, Texas

Peter E. Malin, Ph.D.
Professor of Geology
Division of Earth and Ocean Sciences
Duke University
Durham, North Carolina

Karen J. Meech, Ph.D.
Associate Astronomer
Institute for Astronomy
University of Hawaii
Honolulu, Hawaii

Robert J. Sager
Chair and Professor of Earth Sciences
Pierce College
Lakewood, Washington

Lab Writers

Kenneth Creese
Science Teacher
White Mountain Junior High School
Rock Springs, Wyoming

Linda A. Culp
Science Teacher and Dept. Chair
Thorndale High School
Thorndale, Texas

Bruce M. Jones
Science Teacher and Dept. Chair
The Blake School
Minneapolis, Minnesota

Shannon Miller
Science and Math Teacher
Llano Junior High School
Llano, Texas

Robert Stephen Ricks
Special Services Teacher
Department of Classroom Improvement
Alabama State Department of Education
Montgomery, Alabama

James J. Secosky
Science Teacher
Bloomfield Central School
Bloomfield, New York

Academic Reviewers

Mead Allison, Ph.D.
Assistant Professor of Oceanography
Texas A&M University
Galveston, Texas

Alissa Arp, Ph.D.
Director and Professor of Environmental Studies
Romberg Tiburon Center
San Francisco State University
Tiburon, California

Paul D. Asimow, Ph.D.
Assistant Professor of Geology and Geochemistry
Department of Physics and Planetary Sciences
California Institute of Technology
Pasadena, California

G. Fritz Benedict, Ph.D.
Senior Research Scientist and Astronomer
McDonald Observatory
The University of Texas
Austin, Texas

Russell M. Brengelman, Ph.D.
Professor of Physics
Morehead State University
Morehead, Kentucky

John A. Brockhaus, Ph.D.
Director—Mapping, Charting, and Geodesy Program
Department of Geography and Environmental Engineering
United States Military Academy
West Point, New York

Michael Brown, Ph.D.
Assistant Professor of Planetary Astronomy
Department of Physics and Astronomy
California Institute of Technology
Pasadena, California

Wesley N. Colley, Ph.D.
Postdoctoral Fellow
Harvard-Smithsonian Center for Astrophysics
Cambridge, Massachusetts

Andrew J. Davis, Ph.D.
Manager—ACE Science Data Center
Physics Department
California Institute of Technology
Pasadena, California

Peter E. Demmin, Ed.D.
Former Science Teacher and Department Chair
Amherst Central High School
Amherst, New York

James Denbow, Ph.D.
Associate Professor
Department of Anthropology
The University of Texas
Austin, Texas

Roy W. Hann, Jr., Ph.D.
Professor of Civil Engineering
Texas A&M University
College Station, Texas

Frederick R. Heck, Ph.D.
Professor of Geology
Ferris State University
Big Rapids, Michigan

Richard Hey, Ph.D.
Professor of Geophysics
Hawaii Institute of Geophysics and Planetology
University of Hawaii
Honolulu, Hawaii

John E. Hoover, Ph.D.
Associate Professor of Biology
Millersville University
Millersville, Pennsylvania

Robert W. Houghton, Ph.D.
Senior Staff Associate
Lamont-Doherty Earth Observatory
Columbia University
Palisades, New York

Steven A. Jennings, Ph.D.
Assistant Professor
Department of Geography & Environmental Studies
University of Colorado
Colorado Springs, Colorado

Eric L. Johnson, Ph.D.
Assistant Professor of Geology
Central Michigan University
Mount Pleasant, Michigan

John Kermond, Ph.D.
Visiting Scientist
NOAA–Office of Global Programs
Silver Spring, Maryland

Zavareh Kothavala, Ph.D.
Postdoctoral Associate Scientist
Department of Geology and Geophysics
Yale University
New Haven, Connecticut

Karen Kwitter, Ph.D.
Ebenezer Fitch Professor of Astronomy
Williams College
Williamstown, Massachusetts

Valerie Lang, Ph.D.
Project Leader of Environmental Programs
The Aerospace Corporation
Los Angeles, California

Philip LaRoe
Professor
Helena College of Technology
Helena, Montana

Julie Lutz, Ph.D.
Astronomy Program
Washington State University
Pullman, Washington

Duane F. Marble, Ph.D.
Professor Emeritus
Department of Geography and Natural Resources
Ohio State University
Columbus, Ohio

Joseph A. McClure, Ph.D.
Associate Professor
Department of Physics
Georgetown University
Washington, D.C.

Frank K. McKinney, Ph.D.
Professor of Geology
Appalachian State University
Boone, North Carolina

Joann Mossa, Ph.D.
Associate Professor of Geography
University of Florida
Gainesville, Florida

LaMoine L. Motz, Ph.D.
Coordinator of Science Education
Department of Learning Services
Oakland County Schools
Waterford, Michigan

Barbara Murck, Ph.D.
Assistant Professor of Earth Science
Erindale College
University of Toronto
Mississauga, Ontario, Canada

Hilary Clement Olson, Ph.D.
Research Associate
Institute for Geophysics
The University of Texas
Austin, Texas

Andre Potochnik
Geologist
Grand Canyon Field Institute
Flagstaff, Arizona

John R. Reid, Ph.D.
Professor Emeritus
Department of Geology and Geological Engineering
University of North Dakota
Grand Forks, North Dakota

Gary Rottman, Ph.D.
Associate Director
Laboratory for Atmosphere and Space Physics
University of Colorado
Boulder, Colorado

Dork L. Sahagian, Ph.D.
Professor
Institute for the Study of Earth, Oceans, and Space
University of New Hampshire
Durham, New Hampshire

Peter Sheridan, Ph.D.
Professor of Chemistry
Colgate University
Hamilton, New York

David Sprayberry, Ph.D.
Assistant Director for Observing Support
W.M. Keck Observatory
California Association for Research in Astronomy
Kamuela, Hawaii

Lynne Talley, Ph.D.
Professor
Scripps Institution of Oceanography
University of California
La Jolla, California

Acknowledgments (cont.)

Glenn Thompson, Ph.D.
Scientist
Geophysical Institute
University of Alaska
Fairbanks, Alaska

Martin VanDyke, Ph.D.
Professor of Chemistry, Emeritus
Front Range Community
College
Westminister, Colorado

Thad A. Wasklewicz, Ph.D.
Assistant Professor of Geography
University of Memphis
Memphis, Tennessee

Hans Rudolf Wenk, Ph.D.
Professor of Geology and Geophysical Sciences
University of California
Berkeley, California

Lisa D. White, Ph.D.
Associate Professor of Geosciences
San Francisco State University
San Francisco, California

Lorraine W. Wolf, Ph.D.
Associate Professor of Geology
Auburn University
Auburn, Alabama

Charles A. Wood, Ph.D.
Chairman and Professor of Space Studies
University of North Dakota
Grand Forks, North Dakota

Safety Reviewer

Jack Gerlovich, Ph.D.
Associate Professor
School of Education
Drake University
Des Moines, Iowa

Teacher Reviewers

Barry L. Bishop
Science Teacher and Dept. Chair
San Rafael Junior High School
Ferron, Utah

Yvonne Brannum
Science Teacher and Dept. Chair
Hine Junior High School
Washington, D.C.

Daniel L. Bugenhagen
Science Teacher and Dept. Chair
Yutan Junior & Senior High
School
Yutan, Nebraska

Kenneth Creese
Science Teacher
White Mountain Junior High
School
Rock Springs, Wyoming

Linda A. Culp
Science Teacher and Dept. Chair
Thorndale High School
Thorndale, Texas

Alonda Droege
Science Teacher
Pioneer Middle School
Steilacom, Washington

Laura Fleet
Science Teacher
Alice B. Landrum Middle
School
Ponte Vedra Beach, Florida

Susan Gorman
Science Teacher
Northridge Middle School
North Richland Hills, Texas

C. John Graves
Science Teacher
Monforton Middle School
Bozeman, Montana

Janel Guse
Science Teacher and Dept. Chair
West Central Middle School
Hartford, South Dakota

Gary Habeeb
Science Mentor
Sierra–Plumas Joint Unified
School District
Downieville, California

Dennis Hanson
Science Teacher and Dept. Chair
Big Bear Middle School
Big Bear Lake, California

Norman E. Holcomb
Science Teacher
Marion Local Schools
Maria Stein, Ohio

Tracy Jahn
Science Teacher
Berkshire Junior-Senior High
School
Canaan, New York

David D. Jones
Science Teacher
Andrew Jackson Middle School
Cross Lanes, West Virginia

Howard A. Knodle
Science Teacher
Belvidere High School
Belvidere, Illinois

Michael E. Kral
Science Teacher
West Hardin Middle School
Cecilia, Kentucky

Kathy LaRoe
Science Teacher
East Valley Middle School
East Helena, Montana

Scott Mandel, Ph.D.
Director and Educational Consultant
Teachers Helping Teachers
Los Angeles, California

Kathy McKee
Science Teacher
Hoyt Middle School
Des Moines, Iowa

Michael Minium
Vice President of Program Development
United States Orienteering
Federation
Forest Park, Georgia

Jan Nelson
Science Teacher
East Valley Middle School
East Helena, Montana

Dwight C. Patton
Science Teacher
Carroll T. Welch Middle
School
Horizon City, Texas

Joseph Price
Chairman—Science Department
H. M. Brown Junior High
School
Washington, D.C.

Terry J. Rakes
Science Teacher
Elmwood Junior High School
Rogers, Arkansas

Steven Ramig
Science Teacher
West Point High School
West Point, Nebraska

Helen P. Schiller
Science Teacher
Northwood Middle School
Taylors, South Carolina

Bert J. Sherwood
Science Teacher
Socorro Middle School
El Paso, Texas

Larry Tackett
Science Teacher and Dept. Chair
Andrew Jackson Middle School
Cross Lanes, West Virginia

Walter Woolbaugh
Science Teacher
Manhattan Junior High School
Manhattan, Montana

Alexis S. Wright
Middle School Science Coordinator
Rye Country Day School
Rye, New York

Gordon Zibelman
Science Teacher
Drexel Hill Middle School
Drexel Hill, Pennsylvania

Weather and Climate

Skills Development

Process Skills

QuickLabs

Chapter Labs

Research and Critical Thinking Skills

Apply

Feature Articles

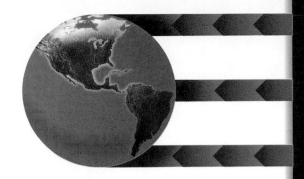

Connections

Chemistry Connection

Mathematics

To the Student

This book was created to make your science experience interesting, exciting, and fun!

Go for It!

Science is a process of discovery, a trek into the unknown. The skills you develop using *Holt Science & Technology*— such as observing, experimenting, and explaining observations and ideas— are the skills you will need for the future. There is a universe of exploration and discovery awaiting those who accept the challenges of science.

Science & Technology

You see the interaction between science and technology every day. Science makes technology possible. On the other hand, some of the products of technology, such as computers, are used to make further scientific discoveries. In fact, much of the scientific work that is done today has become so technically complicated and expensive that no one person can do it entirely alone. But make no mistake, the creative ideas for even the most highly technical and expensive scientific work still come from individuals.

Activities and Labs

The activities and labs in this book will allow you to make some basic but important scientific discoveries on your own. You can even do some exploring on your own at home! Here's your chance to use your imagination and curiosity as you investigate your world.

Keep a ScienceLog

In this book, you will be asked to keep a type of journal called a ScienceLog to record your thoughts, observations, experiments, and conclusions. As you develop your ScienceLog, you will see your own ideas taking shape over time. You'll have a written record of how your ideas have changed as you learn about and explore interesting topics in science.

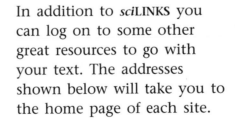

Know "What You'll Do"

The "What You'll Do" list at the beginning of each section is your built-in guide to what you need to learn in each chapter. When you can answer the questions in the Section Review and Chapter Review, you know you are ready for a test.

Check Out the Internet

You will see this  logo throughout the book. You'll be using sciLINKS as your gateway to the Internet. Once you log on to sciLINKS using your computer's Internet link, type in the sciLINKS address. When asked for the keyword code, type in the keyword for that topic. A wealth of resources is now at your disposal to help you learn more about that topic.

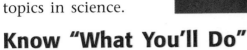

In addition to sciLINKS you can log on to some other great resources to go with your text. The addresses shown below will take you to the home page of each site.

---

 internet**connect**

This textbook contains the following on-line resources to help you make the most of your science experience.

go. hrw .com	SC**LINKS** NSTA	Smithsonian Institution® Internet Connections	CNN**fyi**.com
Visit **go.hrw.com** for extra help and study aids matched to your textbook. Just type in the keyword HST HOME.	Visit **www.scilinks.org** to find resources specific to topics in your textbook. Keywords appear throughout your book to take you further.	Visit **www.si.edu/hrw** for specifically chosen on-line materials from one of our nation's premier science museums.	Visit **www.cnnfyi.com** for late-breaking news and current events stories selected just for you.

The Atmosphere

Pre-Reading
Questions

1. What is air made of?
2. How is the atmosphere
   organized?
3. What is wind and how
   does it move?

FLOATING ON AIR

These skydivers might have checked their parachutes at least a half dozen times before they jumped. They probably also paid particular attention to the day's weather report. Skydivers should know what to expect from the atmosphere. The atmosphere can be unpredictable and dangerous, but it also provides us with the gases needed for our survival on Earth. In this chapter, you will learn about the Earth's atmosphere and how it affects your life.

START-UP
Activity

AIR—IT'S MASSIVE

In this activity, you will find out if air has mass.

Procedure

1. Use a **scale** to find the mass of a **ball,** such as a football or a basketball, with no air in it. Record the mass of the empty ball in your ScienceLog.

2. Pump up the ball with an **air pump.**

3. Use the scale to find the mass of the ball filled with air. Record the mass of the ball filled with air in your ScienceLog.

Analysis

4. Compare the mass of the empty ball with the mass of the ball filled with air. Did the mass of the ball change after you pumped it up?

5. Based on your results, does air have mass? Explain your answer.

Terms to Learn

atmosphere   stratosphere
air pressure   ozone
altitude   mesosphere
troposphere   thermosphere

What You'll Do

◆ Discuss the composition of the Earth's atmosphere.
◆ Explain why pressure changes with altitude.
◆ Explain how temperature changes with altitude.
◆ Describe the layers of the atmosphere.

Characteristics of the Atmosphere

If you were lost in the desert, you could survive for a few days without food and water. But you wouldn't last more than 5 minutes without the *atmosphere*. The **atmosphere** is a mixture of gases that surrounds the Earth. In addition to containing the oxygen we need to breathe, it protects us from the sun's harmful rays. But the atmosphere is always changing. Every breath we take, every tree we plant, and every motor vehicle we ride in affects the composition of our atmosphere. Later you will find out how the atmosphere is changing. But first you need to learn about the atmosphere's composition and structure.

Composition of the Atmosphere

Figure 1 shows the relative amounts of the gases that make up the atmosphere. Besides gases, the atmosphere also contains small amounts of solids and liquids. Tiny solid particles, such as dust, volcanic ash, sea salt, dirt, and smoke, are carried in the air. Next time you turn off the lights at night, shine a flashlight and you will see some of these tiny particles floating in the air. The most common liquid in the atmosphere is water. Liquid water is found as water droplets in clouds. Water vapor, which is also found in the atmosphere, is a gas and is not visible.

Figure 1 *Two gases—nitrogen and oxygen—make up 99 percent of the air we breathe.*

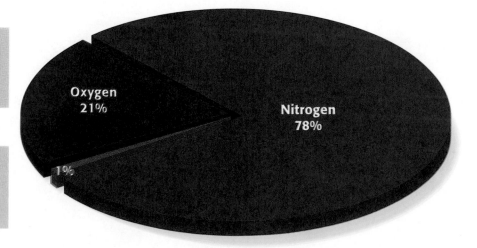

Nitrogen is the most abundant gas in the atmosphere. It is released into the atmosphere by volcanic eruptions and when dead plants and dead animals decay.

Oxygen, the second most common gas in the atmosphere, is produced mainly by plantlike protist and plants.

The **remaining 1 percent** of the atmosphere is made up of argon, carbon dioxide, water vapor, and other gases.

Oxygen
21%

Nitrogen
78%

1%

Atmospheric Pressure and Temperature

Have you ever been in an elevator in a tall building? If you have, you probably remember the "popping" in your ears as you went up or down. As you move up or down in an elevator, the air pressure outside your ears changes, while the air pressure inside your ears stays the same. **Air pressure** is the measure of the force with which the air molecules push on a surface. Your ears pop when the pressure inside and outside of your ears suddenly becomes equal. Air pressure changes throughout the atmosphere. Temperature and the kinds of gases present also change. Why do these changes occur? Read on to find out.

Pressure Think of air pressure as a human pyramid, as shown in **Figure 2.** The people at the bottom of the pyramid can feel all the weight and pressure of the people on top. The person on top doesn't feel any weight because there isn't anyone above. The atmosphere works in a similar way.

The Earth's atmosphere is held around the planet by gravity. Gravity pulls the gas molecules in the atmosphere toward the Earth's surface, giving them weight. This weight causes the air to push against the Earth's surface. As you move farther away from the Earth's surface, air pressure decreases because fewer gas molecules are pushing on you. **Altitude** is the height of an object above the Earth's surface. As altitude increases, air pressure decreases.

Figure 2 *Like the bottom row of the human pyramid, the lower atmosphere experiences greater pressure than the upper atmosphere.*

Air Temperature Air temperature also changes as you increase altitude. As you pass through the atmosphere, air temperature changes between warmer and colder conditions. The temperature differences result mainly from the way solar energy is absorbed as it moves downward through the atmosphere. Some parts of the atmosphere are warmer because they contain gases that absorb solar energy. Other parts do not contain these gases and are therefore cooler.

Layers of the Atmosphere

Based on temperature changes, the Earth's atmosphere is divided into four layers—the troposphere, stratosphere, mesosphere, and thermosphere. **Figure 3** illustrates the four atmospheric layers, showing their altitude and temperature. As you can see, each layer has unique characteristics.

Figure 3 Profile of the Earth's Atmosphere

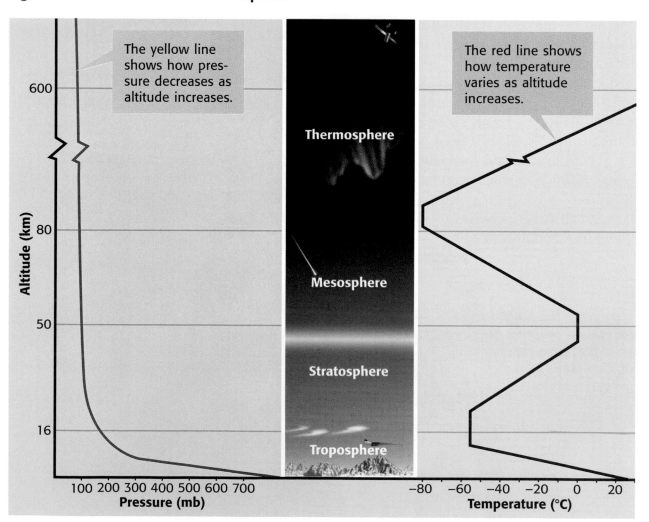

The yellow line shows how pressure decreases as altitude increases.

The red line shows how temperature varies as altitude increases.

Thermosphere

Mesosphere

Stratosphere

Troposphere

Altitude (km): 600, 80, 50, 16

Pressure (mb): 100 200 300 400 500 600 700

Temperature (°C): −80 −60 −40 −20 0 20

Troposphere The **troposphere,** which lies next to the Earth's surface, is the lowest layer of the atmosphere. The troposphere is also the densest atmospheric layer, containing almost 90 percent of the atmosphere's total mass. Almost all of Earth's carbon dioxide, water vapor, clouds, air pollution, weather, and life-forms are found in the troposphere. In fact, the troposphere is the layer in which you live. **Figure 4** shows the effects of altitude on temperature in the troposphere.

Stratosphere The atmospheric layer above the troposphere is called the **stratosphere.** In the stratosphere, the air is very thin and contains little moisture. The lower stratosphere is extremely cold, measuring about –60°C. In the stratosphere, the temperature rises with increasing altitude. This occurs because of ozone. **Ozone** is a molecule that is made up of three oxygen atoms, as shown in **Figure 5.** Almost all of the ozone in the atmosphere is contained in the *ozone layer* of the stratosphere. Ozone absorbs solar energy in the form of ultraviolet radiation, warming the air. By absorbing the ultraviolet radiation, the ozone layer also protects life at the Earth's surface.

Figure 4 *Snow can remain year-round on a mountain top. That is because as altitude increases, the atmosphere thins, losing its ability to absorb and transfer thermal energy.*

Oxygen gas (O$_2$)   Ozone (O$_3$)

Figure 5 *While ozone is made up of three oxygen atoms, the oxygen in the air you breathe is made up of two oxygen atoms.*

APPLY

UV and SPFs

People protect themselves from the sun's damaging rays by applying sunblock. Exposure of unprotected skin to the sun's ultraviolet rays over a long period of time can cause skin cancer. The breakdown of the Earth's ozone layer is thinning the layer, which allows some harmful ultraviolet radiation to reach the Earth's surface. Sunblocks contain different ratings of SPFs, or skin protection factors. What do the SPF ratings mean?

Mesosphere   Above the stratosphere is the mesosphere. The **mesosphere** is the coldest layer of the atmosphere. As in the troposphere, the temperature drops with increasing altitude. Temperatures can be as low as –93°C at the top of the mesosphere. Scientists have recently discovered large wind storms in the mesosphere with winds reaching speeds of more than 320 km/h.

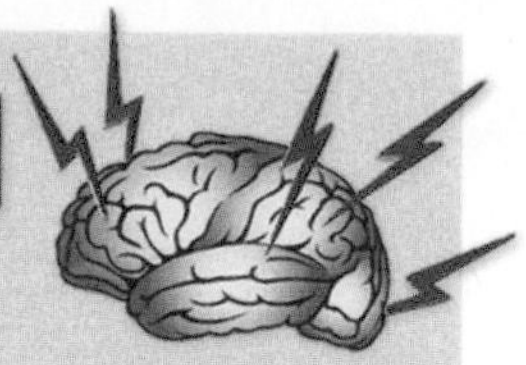

Thermosphere   The uppermost atmospheric layer is the **thermosphere.** Here temperature again increases with altitude because many of the gases are absorbing solar radiation. Temperatures in this layer can reach 1,700°C.

When you think of an area with high temperatures, you probably think of a place that is very hot. While the thermosphere has very high temperatures, it would not feel hot. Temperature and heat are not the same thing. Temperature is a measure of the average energy of particles in motion. A high temperature means that the particles are moving very fast. Heat, on the other hand, is the transfer of energy between objects at different temperatures. But in order to transfer energy, particles must touch one another. **Figure 6** illustrates how the density of particles affects the heating of the atmosphere.

Figure 6 *Temperatures in the thermosphere are higher than those in the troposphere, but the air particles are too far apart for energy to be transferred.*

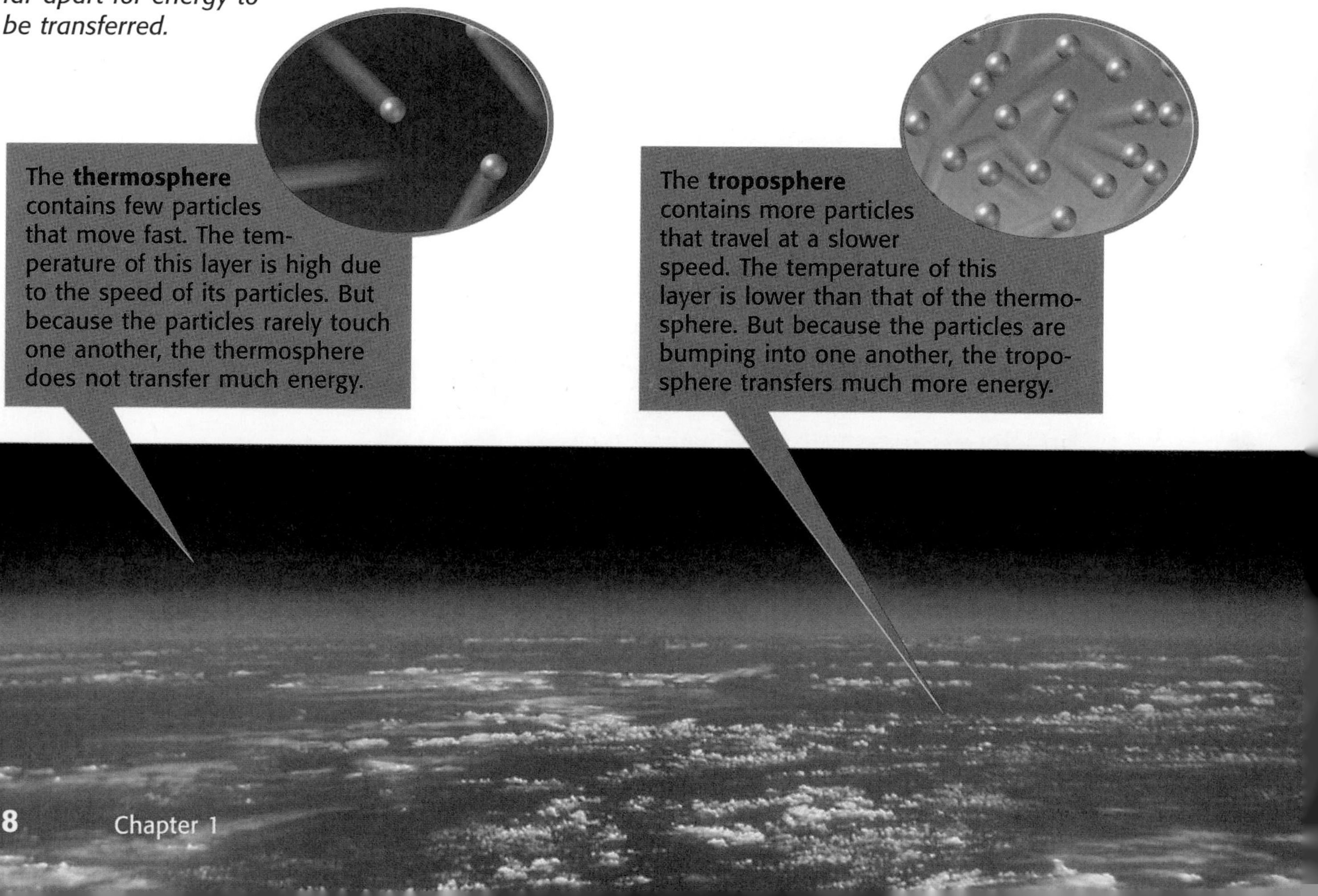

The **thermosphere** contains few particles that move fast. The temperature of this layer is high due to the speed of its particles. But because the particles rarely touch one another, the thermosphere does not transfer much energy.

The **troposphere** contains more particles that travel at a slower speed. The temperature of this layer is lower than that of the thermosphere. But because the particles are bumping into one another, the troposphere transfers much more energy.

Ionosphere In the upper part of the mesosphere and the lower thermosphere, nitrogen and oxygen atoms absorb harmful solar energy, such as X rays and gamma rays. This absorption not only contributes to the thermosphere's high temperatures but also causes the gas particles to become electrically charged. Electrically charged particles are called ions; therefore, this part of the thermosphere is referred to as the *ionosphere*. Sometimes these ions radiate energy as light of different colors, as shown in **Figure 7.**

Figure 7 *Aurora borealis (northern lights) and aurora australis (southern lights) occur in the ionosphere.*

The ionosphere also reflects certain radio waves, such as AM radio waves. If you have ever listened to an AM radio station, you can be sure that the ionosphere had something to do with how clear it sounded. When conditions are right, an AM radio wave can travel around the world after being reflected off the ionosphere. These radio signals bounce off the ionosphere and are sent back to Earth.

SECTION REVIEW

1. Explain why pressure decreases but temperature varies as altitude increases.

2. What causes air pressure?

3. How can the thermosphere have high temperatures but not feel hot?

4. **Analyzing Relationships** Identify one characteristic of each layer of the atmosphere, and explain how that characteristic affects life on Earth.

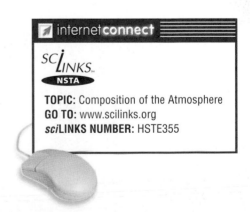

internet**connect**

SC*L*INKS.
NSTA

TOPIC: Composition of the Atmosphere
GO TO: www.scilinks.org
*sci*LINKS NUMBER: HSTE355

Terms to Learn

radiation
conduction
convection
greenhouse effect
global warming

What You'll Do

◆ Describe what happens to radiation that reaches the Earth.

◆ Summarize the processes of radiation, conduction, and convection.

◆ Explain how the greenhouse effect could contribute to global warming.

Heating of the Atmosphere

Have you ever walked barefoot across a sidewalk on a sunny day? If so, your foot felt the warmth of the hot pavement. How did the sidewalk become so warm? The sidewalk was heated as it absorbed the sun's energy. The Earth's atmosphere is also heated in several ways by the transfer of energy from the sun. In this section you will find out what happens to the solar energy as it enters the Earth's atmosphere, how the energy is transferred through the atmosphere, and why it seems to be getting hotter every year.

Energy in the Atmosphere

The Earth receives energy from the sun by radiation. **Radiation** is the transfer of energy as electromagnetic waves. Although the sun releases a huge amount of energy, the Earth receives only about two-billionths of this energy. Yet even this small amount of energy has a very large impact on Earth. **Figure 8** shows what happens to all this energy once it enters the atmosphere.

When energy is absorbed by a surface, it heats that surface. For example, when you stand in the sun on a cool day, you can feel the sun's rays warming your body. Your skin

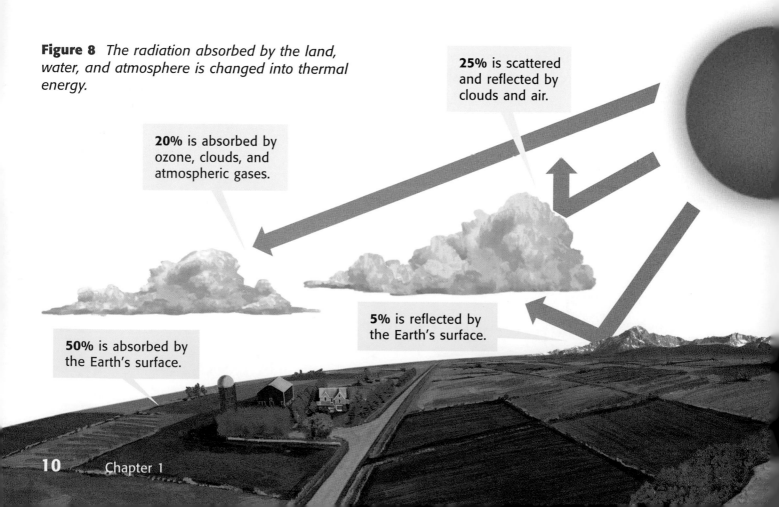

Figure 8 *The radiation absorbed by the land, water, and atmosphere is changed into thermal energy.*

25% is scattered and reflected by clouds and air.

20% is absorbed by ozone, clouds, and atmospheric gases.

5% is reflected by the Earth's surface.

50% is absorbed by the Earth's surface.

absorbs the radiation, causing your skin's molecules to move faster. You feel this as an increase in temperature. The same thing happens when energy is absorbed by the Earth's surface. The energy from the Earth's surface can then be transferred to the atmosphere, which heats it.

Conduction **Conduction** is the transfer of thermal energy from one material to another by direct contact. Think back to the example about walking barefoot on a hot sidewalk. Conduction occurs when thermal energy is transferred from the sidewalk to your foot. Thermal energy always moves from warm to cold areas. Just as your foot is heated by the sidewalk, the air is heated by land and ocean surfaces. When air molecules come into direct contact with a warm surface, thermal energy is transferred to the atmosphere.

Convection Most thermal energy in the atmosphere moves by *convection*. **Convection** is the transfer of thermal energy by the circulation or movement of a liquid or gas. For instance, as air is heated, it becomes less dense and rises. Cool air is more dense and sinks. As the cool air sinks, it pushes the warm air up. The cool air is eventually heated by the ground and again begins to rise. This continual process of warm air rising and cool air sinking creates a circular movement of air, called a *convection current*, as shown in **Figure 9.**

BRAIN FOOD

If the Earth is continually absorbing solar energy and changing it to thermal energy, why doesn't the Earth get hotter and hotter? The reason is that much of this energy is lost to space. This is especially true on cloudless nights.

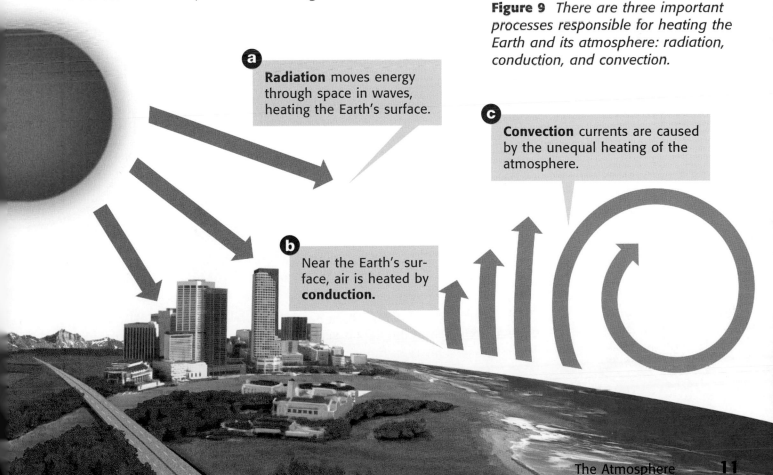

Figure 9 *There are three important processes responsible for heating the Earth and its atmosphere: radiation, conduction, and convection.*

a **Radiation** moves energy through space in waves, heating the Earth's surface.

c **Convection** currents are caused by the unequal heating of the atmosphere.

b Near the Earth's surface, air is heated by **conduction.**

The Greenhouse Effect

As you have already learned, 50 percent of the radiation that enters the Earth's atmosphere is absorbed by the Earth's surface. This energy is then reradiated to the Earth's atmosphere as thermal energy. Gases, such as carbon dioxide and water vapor, can stop this energy from escaping into space by absorbing it and then radiating it back to the Earth. As a result, the Earth's atmosphere stays warm. This is similar to how a blanket keeps you warm at night. The Earth's heating process, in which the gases in the atmosphere trap thermal energy, is known as the **greenhouse effect.** This term is used because the Earth's atmosphere works much like a greenhouse, as shown in **Figure 10.**

Figure 10 *The gases in the atmosphere act like a layer of glass. The gases allow solar energy to pass through. But some of the gases trap thermal energy.*

1 Sunlight streams through the glass into the greenhouse.

2 Sunlight is absorbed by objects inside the greenhouse. The objects radiate the energy as thermal energy.

3 The glass stops the thermal energy from escaping to the outside.

Global Warming Not every gas in the atmosphere traps thermal energy. Those that do trap this energy are called *greenhouse gases.* In recent decades, many scientists have become concerned that an increase of these gases, particularly carbon dioxide, may be causing an increase in the greenhouse effect. These scientists have hypothesized that a rise in carbon dioxide as a result of human activity has led to increased global temperatures. A rise in average global temperatures is called **global warming.** If there were an increase in the greenhouse effect, global warming would result.

The Radiation Balance For the Earth to remain livable, the amount of energy received from the sun and the amount of energy returned to space must be equal. As you saw in Figure 8, about 30 percent of the incoming energy is reflected back into space. Most of the 70 percent that is absorbed by the Earth and its atmosphere is also sent back into space. The balance between incoming energy and outgoing energy is known as the *radiation balance.* If greenhouse gases, such as carbon dioxide, continue to increase in the atmosphere, the radiation balance may be affected. Some of the energy that once escaped into space could be trapped. The Earth's temperatures would continue to rise, causing major changes in plant and animal communities.

Keeping the Earth Livable Some scientists argue that the Earth had warmer periods before humans ever walked the planet, so global warming may be a natural process. Nevertheless, many of the world's nations have signed a treaty to reduce activities that increase greenhouse gases in the atmosphere. Another step that is being taken to reduce high carbon dioxide levels in the atmosphere is the planting of millions of trees by volunteers, as shown in **Figure 11.**

Figure 11 *Plants take in harmful carbon dioxide and give off oxygen, which we need to breathe.*

SECTION REVIEW

1. Describe three things that can happen to energy when it reaches the Earth's atmosphere.

2. How is energy transferred through the atmosphere?

3. What is the greenhouse effect?

4. **Inferring Relationships** How does the process of convection rely on conduction?

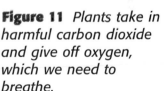

internetconnect

SC*i*LINKS
NSTA

TOPIC: Energy in the Atmosphere
GO TO: www.scilinks.org
***sci*LINKS NUMBER:** HSTE360

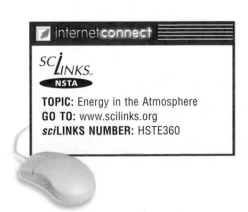

Terms to Learn

wind   westerlies
Coriolis effect   polar easterlies
trade winds   jet streams

What You'll Do

◆ Explain the relationship between air pressure and wind direction.
◆ Describe the global patterns of wind.
◆ Explain the causes of local wind patterns.

Atmospheric Pressure and Winds

Sometimes it cools you. Other times it scatters tidy piles of newly swept trash. Still other times it uproots trees and flattens buildings, as shown in **Figure 12. Wind** is moving air. In this section you will learn about air movement and about the similarities and differences between different kinds of winds.

Figure 12 *In 1998, the winds from Hurricane Mitch reached speeds of 288 km/h, destroying entire towns in Honduras.*

Why Air Moves

Wind is created by differences in air pressure. The greater the pressure difference is, the faster the wind moves. This difference in air pressure is generally caused by the unequal heating of the Earth. For example, the air at the equator is warmer and less dense. This warm, less-dense air rises. As it rises it creates an area of low pressure. At the poles, however, the air is colder and more dense. Colder, more-dense air is heavier and sinks. This cold, sinking air creates areas of high pressure. Pressure differences in the atmosphere at the equator and at the poles cause air to move. Because air moves from areas of high pressure to areas of low pressure, winds generally move from the poles to the equator, as shown in **Figure 13.**

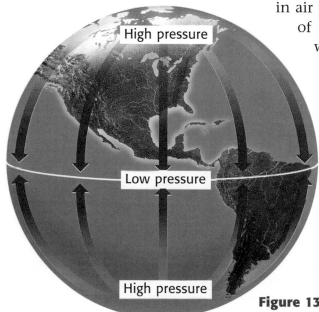

High pressure

Low pressure

High pressure

Figure 13 *Surface winds blow from polar high-pressure areas to equatorial low-pressure areas.*

Pressure Belts You may be imagining wind moving in one huge, circular pattern, from the poles to the equator. In fact, the pattern is much more complex. As warm air rises over the equator, it begins to cool. Eventually, it stops rising and moves toward the poles. At about 30° north and 30° south latitude, some of the cool air begins to sink. This cool, sinking air causes a high pressure belt near 30° north and 30° south latitude.

At the poles, cold air sinks. As this air moves away from the poles and along the Earth's surface, it begins to warm. As the air warms, the pressure drops, creating a low-pressure belt around 60° north and 60° south latitude. The circular patterns caused by the rising and sinking of air are called *convection cells,* as shown in **Figure 14.**

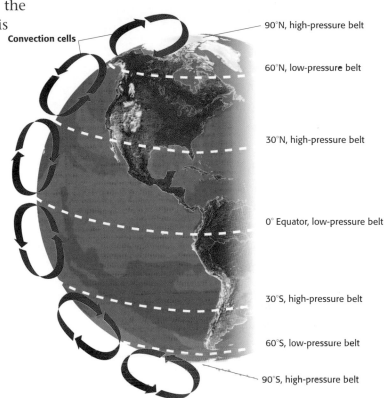

Convection cells

90°N, high-pressure belt
60°N, low-pressure belt
30°N, high-pressure belt
0° Equator, low-pressure belt
30°S, high-pressure belt
60°S, low-pressure belt
90°S, high-pressure belt

Figure 14 *The uneven heating of the Earth produces pressure belts. These belts occur at about every 30° of latitude.*

Coriolis Effect Winds don't blow directly north or south. The movement of wind is affected by the rotation of the Earth. The Earth's rotation causes wind to travel in a curved path rather than in a straight line. The curving of moving objects, such as wind, by the Earth's rotation is called the **Coriolis effect.** Because of the Coriolis effect, the winds in the Northern Hemisphere curve to the right, and those in the Southern Hemisphere curve to the left.

To better understand how the Coriolis effect works, imagine rolling a marble across a Lazy Susan while it is spinning. What you might observe is shown in **Figure 15.**

Direction of rotation

Actual path

Intended path

Figure 15 *Because of the Lazy Susan's rotation, the path of the marble curves instead of traveling in a straight line. The Earth's rotation affects objects traveling on or near its surface in much the same way.*

The Atmosphere

Types of Winds

There are two main types of winds: local winds and global winds. Both types are caused by the uneven heating of the Earth's surface and by pressure differences. *Local winds* generally move short distances and can blow from any direction. *Global winds* are part of a pattern of air circulation that moves across the Earth. These winds travel longer distances than local winds, and they each travel in a specific direction. **Figure 16** shows the location and movement of major global wind systems. First let's review the different types of global winds, and later in this section we will discuss local winds.

Trade Winds   In both hemispheres, the winds that blow from 30° latitude to the equator are called **trade winds.** The Coriolis effect causes the trade winds to curve, as shown in Figure 16. Early traders used the trade winds to sail from Europe to the Americas. This is how they became known as "trade winds."

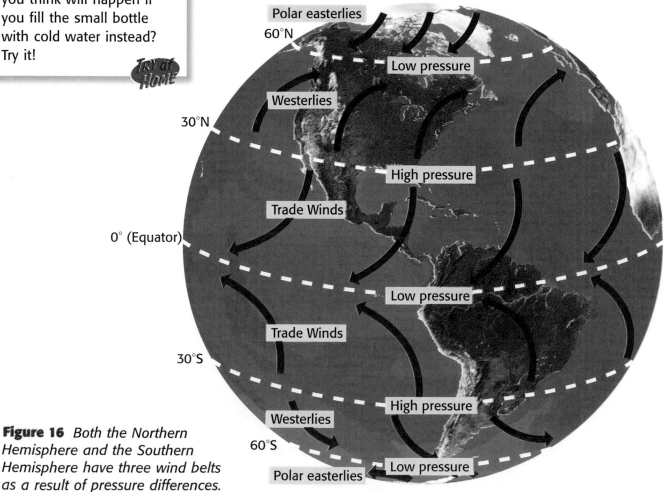

Figure 16 *Both the Northern Hemisphere and the Southern Hemisphere have three wind belts as a result of pressure differences.*

The Doldrums and Horse Latitudes The trade winds of the Northern and Southern Hemispheres meet in an area of low pressure around the equator called the *doldrums*. In the doldrums there is very little wind because of the warm rising air. *Doldrums* comes from an Old English word meaning "foolish." Sailors were considered foolish if they got their ship stuck in these areas of little wind.

At about 30° north and 30° south latitude, sinking air creates an area of high pressure. This area is called the *horse latitudes*. Here the winds are weak. Legend has it that the name horse latitudes was given to these areas when sailing ships carried horses from Europe to the Americas. When the ships were stuck in this area due to lack of wind, horses were sometimes thrown overboard to save drinking water for the sailors.

Westerlies The **westerlies** are wind belts found in both the Northern and Southern Hemispheres between 30° and 60° latitude. The westerlies flow toward the poles in the opposite direction of the trade winds. The westerlies helped early traders return to Europe. Sailing ships, like the one in **Figure 17,** were designed to best use the wind to move the ship forward.

Environment
CONNECTION

Humans have been using wind energy for thousands of years. Today wind energy is being tapped to produce electricity at wind farms. Wind farms are made up of hundreds of wind turbines that look like giant airplane propellers attached to towers. Together these wind turbines can produce enough electricity for an entire town.

Figure 17 *This ship is a replica of Columbus's Santa Maria. If it had not sunk, the Santa Maria would have used the westerlies to return to Europe.*

Polar Easterlies The **polar easterlies** are wind belts that extend from the poles to 60° latitude in both hemispheres. The polar easterlies are formed from cold, sinking air moving from the poles toward 60° north and 60° south latitude.

To find out how to build a device that measures wind speed, turn to page 102 of the LabBook.

Jet Streams The **jet streams** are narrow belts of high-speed winds that blow in the upper troposphere and lower stratosphere, as shown in **Figure 18.** These winds often change speed and can reach maximum speeds of 500 km/h. Unlike other global winds, the jet streams do not follow regular paths around the Earth.

Knowing the position of the jet stream is important to both meteorologists and airline pilots. Because the jet stream controls the movement of storms, meteorologists can track a storm if they know the location of the jet stream. By flying in the direction of the jet stream, pilots can save time and fuel.

Local Winds Local winds are influenced by the geography of an area. An area's geography, such as a shoreline or a mountain, sometimes produces temperature differences that cause local winds like land and sea breezes, as shown in **Figure 19.** During the day, land heats up faster than water. The land heats the air above it. At night, land cools faster than water, cooling the air above the land.

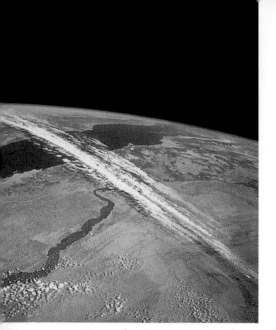

Figure 18 *The jet stream is the white stripe moving diagonally above the Earth.*

Figure 19 Sea and Land Breezes

Warm air

As warm air rises, it creates an area of low pressure over the land.

The cool air moves toward the land, producing a *sea breeze.*

Cool air

Air over the water is cooler and creates an area of high pressure.

Cool air

Air over land is cooler and creates an area of high pressure.

The cool air moves toward the water, producing a *land breeze.*

Warm air

Air over the water is warmer and creates an area of low pressure.

Mountain and valley breezes are another example of local winds caused by an area's geography. Campers in mountain areas may feel a warm afternoon change into a cold night soon after the sun sets. The illustrations in **Figure 20** show you why.

MATH BREAK

Calculating Groundspeed
An airplane has an airspeed of 500 km/h and is moving into a 150 km/h head wind due to the jet stream. What is the actual groundspeed of the plane? Over a 3-hour flight, how far would the plane actually travel? (Hint: To calculate actual ground-speed, subtract head-wind speed from airspeed.)

Warm air

During the day, the sun heats the valley floor and warms the air above it.

Warm air from the valley moves upslope, creating a *valley breeze*.

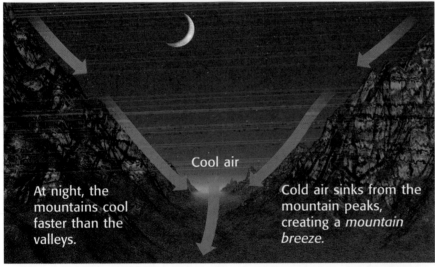

Cool air

At night, the mountains cool faster than the valleys.

Cold air sinks from the mountain peaks, creating a *mountain breeze*.

Figure 20 *During the day, a gentle breeze blows up the slopes. At night, cold air flows downslope and settles in the valley.*

SECTION REVIEW

1. How does the Coriolis effect affect wind movement?

2. What causes winds?

3. Compare and contrast global winds and local winds.

4. **Applying Concepts** Suppose you are vacationing at the beach. It is daytime and you want to go swimming in the ocean. You know the beach is near your hotel, but you don't know what direction it is in. How might the local wind help you find the ocean?

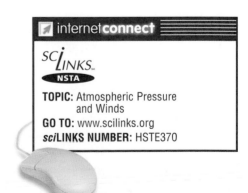

Terms to Learn

primary pollutants
secondary pollutants
acid precipitation

What You'll Do

◆ Describe the major types of air pollution.
◆ Name the major causes of air pollution.
◆ Explain how air pollution can affect human health.
◆ Explain how air pollution can be reduced.

The Air We Breathe

Air pollution, as shown in **Figure 21,** is not a new problem. By the middle of the 1700s, many of the world's large cities suffered from poor air quality. Most of the pollutants were released from factories and homes that burned coal for energy. Even 2,000 years ago, the Romans were complaining about the bad air in their cities. At that time the air was thick with the smoke from fires and the smell of open sewers. So you see, cities have always been troubled with air pollution. In this section you will learn about the different types of air pollution, their sources, and what the world is doing to reduce them.

Figure 21 *The air pollution in Mexico City is sometimes so dangerous that some people wear surgical masks when they go outside.*

Air Quality

Even "clean" air is not perfectly clean. It contains many pollutants from natural sources. These pollutants include dust, sea salt, volcanic gases and ash, smoke from forest fires, pollen, swamp gas, and many other materials. In fact, natural sources produce a greater amount of pollutants than humans do. But we have adapted to many of these natural pollutants.

Most of the air pollution mentioned in the news is a result of human activities. Pollutants caused by human activities can be solids, liquids, or gases. Human-caused air pollution, such as that shown in Figure 21, is most common in cities. As more people move to cities, urban air pollution increases.

Types of Air Pollution

Air pollutants are generally described as either *primary pollutants* or *secondary pollutants*. **Primary pollutants** are pollutants that are put directly into the air by human or natural activity. **Figure 22** shows some examples of primary air pollutants.

Figure 22 *Exhaust from vehicles, ash from volcanic eruptions, and soot from smoke are all examples of primary pollutants.*

Secondary pollutants are pollutants that form from chemical reactions that occur when primary pollutants come in contact with other primary pollutants or with naturally occurring substances, such as water vapor. Many secondary pollutants are formed when a primary pollutant reacts with sunlight. Ozone and smog are examples of secondary pollutants. As you read at the beginning of this chapter, ozone is a gas in the stratosphere that is helpful and absorbs harmful rays from the sun. Near the ground, however, ozone is a dangerous pollutant that affects the health of all organisms. Ozone and smog are produced when sunlight reacts with automobile exhaust, as illustrated in **Figure 23.**

Figure 23 *Many large cities suffer from smog, especially those with a sunny climate and millions of automobiles.*

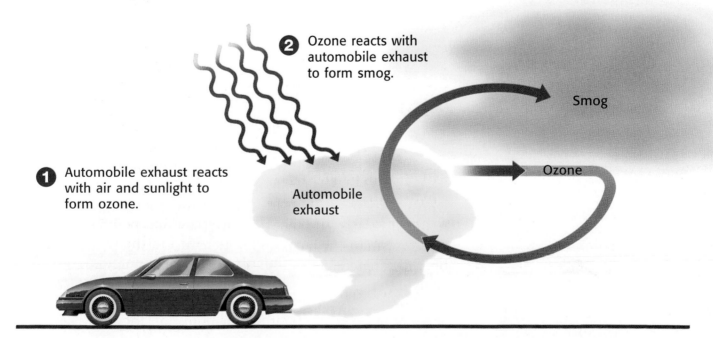

2 Ozone reacts with automobile exhaust to form smog.

Smog

1 Automobile exhaust reacts with air and sunlight to form ozone.

Automobile exhaust

Ozone

Sources of Human-Caused Air Pollution

Human-caused air pollution comes from a variety of sources. The major source of air pollution today is transportation, as shown in **Figure 24.** Cars contribute about 60 percent of the human-caused air pollution in the United States. The oxides that come from car exhaust, such as nitrogen oxide, contribute to smog and acid rain. *Oxides* are chemical compounds that contain oxygen and other elements.

Figure 24 *Seventy percent of the carbon monoxide in the United States is produced by fuel-burning vehicles.*

Industrial Air Pollution Many industrial plants and electric power plants burn fossil fuels to get their energy. But burning fossil fuels causes large amounts of oxides to be released into the air, as shown in **Figure 25.** In fact, the burning of fossil fuels in industrial and electric power plants is responsible for 96 percent of the sulfur oxides released into the atmosphere.

Some industries also produce chemicals that form poisonous fumes. The chemicals used by oil refineries, chemical manufacturing plants, dry-cleaning businesses, furniture refinishers, and auto-body shops can add poisonous fumes to the air.

Figure 25 *This power plant burns coal to get its energy and releases sulfur oxides and particulates into the atmosphere.*

Indoor Air Pollution Air pollution is not limited to the outdoors. Sometimes the air inside a home or building is even worse than the air outside. The air inside a building can be polluted by the compounds found in household cleaners and cooking smoke. The compounds in new carpets, paints, and building materials can also add to indoor air pollution, especially if the windows and doors are tightly sealed to keep energy bills low.

The Air Pollution Problem

Air pollution is both a local and global concern. As you have already learned, local air pollution, such as smog, generally affects large cities. Air pollution becomes a global concern when local pollution moves away from its source. Winds can move pollutants from one place to another, sometimes reducing the amount of pollution in the source area but increasing it in another place. For example, the prevailing winds carry air pollution created in the midwestern United States hundreds of miles to Canada. One such form of this pollution is acid precipitation.

Figure 26 *Acid precipitation can kill living things, such as fish and trees, by making their environment too acidic to live in.*

Acid Precipitation   Precipitation that contains acids from air pollution is called **acid precipitation.** When fossil fuels are burned, they release oxides of sulfur and nitrogen into the atmosphere. When these oxides combine with water droplets in the atmosphere, they form sulfuric acid and nitric acid, which fall as precipitation. Acid precipitation has many negative effects on the environment, as shown in **Figure 26.**

The Ozone Hole   Other global concerns brought about by air pollution include the warming of our planet and the ozone hole in the stratosphere. In the 1970s, scientists determined that some chemicals released into the atmosphere react with ozone in the ozone layer. The reaction results in a breakdown of ozone into oxygen, which does not block the sun's harmful ultraviolet rays. The loss of ozone creates an ozone hole, which allows more ultraviolet rays to reach the Earth's surface. **Figure 27** shows a satellite image of the ozone hole.

Figure 27 *This satellite image, taken in 1998, shows that the ozone hole, the dark blue area, is still growing.*

Effects on Human Health You step outside and notice a smoky haze. When you take a deep breath, your throat tingles and you begin to cough. Air pollution like this affects many cities around the world. For example, on March 17, 1992, in Mexico City, all children under the age of 14 were prohibited from going to school because of extremely high levels of air pollution. This is an extreme case, but daily exposure to small amounts of air pollution can cause serious health problems. Children, elderly people, and people with allergies, lung problems, and heart problems are especially vulnerable to the effects of air pollution. **Figure 28** illustrates some of the effects that air pollution has on the human body.

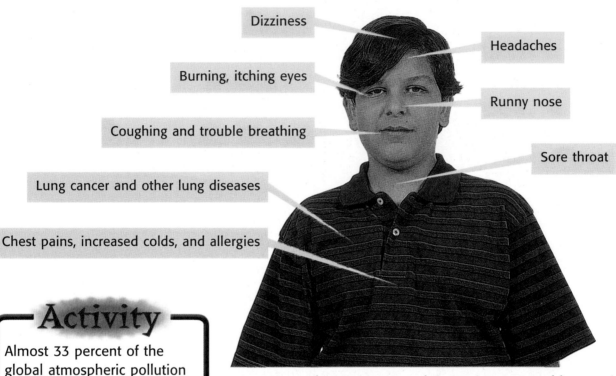

Dizziness

Headaches

Burning, itching eyes

Runny nose

Coughing and trouble breathing

Sore throat

Lung cancer and other lung diseases

Chest pains, increased colds, and allergies

Figure 28 *The Environmental Protection Agency blames air pollution for at least 2,000 new cases of cancer each year.*

Cleaning Up Our Act

Is all this talk about bad air making you a little choked up? Don't worry, help is on the way! In the United States, progress has been made in cleaning up the air. One reason for this progress is the Clean Air Act, which was passed by Congress in 1970. The Clean Air Act is a law that gives the Environmental Protection Agency (EPA) the authority to control the amount of air pollutants that can be released from any source, such as cars and factories. The EPA also checks air quality. If air quality worsens, the EPA can set stricter standards. What are car manufacturers and factories doing to improve air quality? Read on to find out.

Activity

Almost 33 percent of the global atmospheric pollution from carbon dioxide is caused by power plants that burn coal or other fossil fuels. We rely on these sources of power for a better way of life, but our use of them is polluting our air and worsening our quality of life. Use your school library or the Internet to find out about some other sources of electric power. What special problems does each source of energy bring with it?

TRY at Home

Controlling Air Pollution from Vehicles The EPA has required car manufacturers to meet a certain standard for the exhaust that comes out of the tailpipe on cars. New cars now have devices that remove most of the pollutants from the car's exhaust as it exits the tailpipe. Car manufacturers are also making cars that run on fuels other than gasoline. Some of these cars run on hydrogen and natural gas, while others run on batteries powered by solar energy. The car shown in **Figure 29** is electric.

Are electric cars the cure for air pollution? Turn to page 33 and decide for yourself.

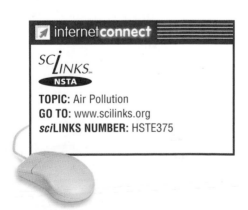

Figure 29 *Instead of having to refuel at a gas station, an electric car is plugged in to a recharging outlet.*

Controlling Air Pollution from Industry The Clean Air Act requires many industries to use scrubbers. A scrubber is a device that attaches to smokestacks to remove some of the more harmful pollutants before they are released into the air. One such scrubber is used in coal-burning power plants in the United States to remove ash and other particles from the smokestacks. Scrubbers prevent 22 million metric tons of ash from being released into the air each year.

Although we have a long way to go, we're taking steps in the right direction to keep the air clean for future generations.

SECTION REVIEW

1. How can the air inside a building be more polluted than the air outside?

2. Why might it be difficult to establish a direct link between air pollution and health problems?

3. How has the Clean Air Act helped to reduce air pollution?

4. **Applying Concepts** How is the water cycle affected by air pollution?

internet**connect**

*sci*LINKS
NSTA

TOPIC: Air Pollution
GO TO: www.scilinks.org
*sci*LINKS NUMBER: HSTE375

Discovery Lab

Under Pressure!

You are planning a picnic with your friends, so you look in the newspaper for the weather forecast. The temperature this afternoon should be in the low 80s. This temperature sounds quite comfortable! But you notice that the newspaper's forecast also includes the barometer reading. What's a barometer? And what does the reading tell you? In this activity, you will build your own barometer and will discover what this tool can tell you.

MATERIALS

- balloon
- scissors
- large empty coffee can, 10 cm in diameter
- masking tape or rubber band
- drinking straw
- transparent tape
- index card

Ask a Question

1 How can I make a tool that measures changes in atmospheric pressure?

Form a Hypothesis

2 In your ScienceLog, write a few sentences that answer the question above.

Conduct an Experiment

3 Stretch and blow up the balloon. Then let the air out. This step will let your barometer be more sensitive to changes in atmospheric pressure.

4 Cut off the end of the balloon that you put in your mouth to blow it up. Stretch the balloon over the mouth of the coffee can. Attach the balloon to the can with the tape or the rubber band.

5 Cut one end of the straw at an angle to make a pointer.

6 Place the straw with the pointer pointed away from the center of the stretched balloon. Look at the illustration below. Place the straw so that 5 cm of the end of the straw hang over the edge of the can. Tape the straw to the balloon.

7 Tape the index card to the can near the straw. Congratulations! You have just made a barometer!

8 Place the barometer outside for 3–4 days. On each day, mark on the index card where the straw points.

Analyze the Results

9 What factors affect how your barometer works? Explain your answer.

10 What does it mean when the straw moves up?

11 What does it mean when the straw moves down?

Draw Conclusions

12 Compare your results with the barometric pressures listed in your local newspaper. What kind of weather is associated with high pressure? What kind of weather is associated with low pressure?

13 Does the barometer you built support your hypothesis? Explain your answer.

Going Further
Now you can calibrate your barometer! Get the weather section from your local newspaper for the same three or four days that you are testing your barometer. Find the barometer reading in the newspaper for each day, and record it beside that day's mark on your index card. Divide the markings on the index card into equal spaces. Write the matching barometric pressures on the card.

Chapter Highlights

SECTION 1

Vocabulary

atmosphere *(p. 4)*

air pressure *(p. 5)*

altitude *(p. 5)*

troposphere *(p. 7)*

stratosphere *(p. 7)*

ozone *(p. 7)*

mesosphere *(p. 8)*

thermosphere *(p. 8)*

Section Notes

- The atmosphere is a mixture of gases.

- Nitrogen and oxygen are the two most abundant atmospheric gases.

- Throughout the atmosphere, there are changes in air pressure, temperature, and gases.

- Air pressure decreases as altitude increases.

- Temperature differences in the atmosphere are a result of the way solar energy is absorbed as it moves downward through the atmosphere.

- The troposphere is the lowest and densest layer of the atmosphere. All weather occurs in the troposphere.

- The stratosphere contains the ozone layer, which protects us from harmful radiation.

- The mesosphere is the coldest layer of the atmosphere.

- The uppermost atmospheric layer is the thermosphere.

SECTION 2

Vocabulary

radiation *(p. 10)*

conduction *(p. 11)*

convection *(p. 11)*

greenhouse effect *(p. 12)*

global warming *(p. 12)*

Section Notes

- The Earth receives energy from the sun by radiation.

- Energy that reaches the Earth's surface is absorbed, reflected, or reradiated.

- Energy is transferred through the atmosphere by conduction and convection.

- The greenhouse effect is caused by gases in the atmosphere that trap thermal energy reflected off and radiated from the Earth's surface.

Labs

Boiling Over! *(p. 100)*

✓ Skills Check

Math Concepts

FLYING AGAINST THE JET STREAM The groundspeed of an airplane can be affected by the jet stream. The jet stream can push an airplane toward its final destination or slow it down. To find the groundspeed of an airplane, you either add or subtract the wind speed, depending on whether the airplane is moving with or against the jet stream. For example, if an airplane is traveling at an airspeed of 400 km/h and is moving with a 100 km/h jet stream, you would add the jet stream speed to the airspeed of the airplane to calculate the groundspeed.

$$400 \text{ km/h} + 100 \text{ km/h} = 500 \text{ km/h}$$

To calculate the groundspeed of an airplane traveling at 400 km/h that is moving into a 100 km/h jet stream, you would subtract the jet-stream speed from the airspeed of the airplane.

$$400 \text{ km/h} - 100 \text{ km/h} = 300 \text{ km/h}$$

Visual Understanding

GLOBAL WINDS Study Figure 16 on page 16 to review the global wind belts that result from air pressure differences.

SECTION 3

Vocabulary

wind *(p. 14)*
Coriolis effect *(p. 15)*
trade winds *(p. 16)*
westerlies *(p. 17)*
polar easterlies *(p. 17)*
jet streams *(p. 18)*

Section Notes

- At the Earth's surface, winds blow from areas of high pressure to areas of low pressure.

- Pressure belts exist approximately every 30° of latitude.

- The Coriolis effect makes wind curve as it moves across the Earth's surface.

- Global winds are part of a pattern of air circulation across the Earth and include the trade winds, the westerlies, and the polar easterlies.

- Local winds move short distances, can blow in any direction, and are influenced by geography.

Labs

Go Fly a Bike! *(p. 102)*

SECTION 4

Vocabulary

primary pollutants *(p. 21)*
secondary pollutants *(p. 21)*
acid precipitation *(p. 23)*

Section Notes

- Air pollutants are generally classified as primary or secondary pollutants.

- Human-caused pollution comes from a variety of sources, including factories, cars, and homes.

- Air pollution can heighten problems associated with allergies, lung problems, and heart problems.

- The Clean Air Act has reduced air pollution by controlling the amount of pollutants that can be released from cars and factories.

---

internet**connect**

GO TO: go.hrw.com

Visit the **HRW** Web site for a variety of learning tools related to this chapter. Just type in the keyword:

KEYWORD: HSTATM

GO TO: www.scilinks.org

Visit the **National Science Teachers Association** on-line Web site for Internet resources related to this chapter. Just type in the *sci*LINKS number for more information about the topic:

TOPIC: Composition of the Atmosphere	*sci*LINKS NUMBER: HSTE355
TOPIC: Energy in the Atmosphere	*sci*LINKS NUMBER: HSTE360
TOPIC: The Greenhouse Effect	*sci*LINKS NUMBER: HSTE365
TOPIC: Atmospheric Pressure and Winds	*sci*LINKS NUMBER: HSTE370
TOPIC: Air Pollution	*sci*LINKS NUMBER: HSTE375

Chapter Review

USING VOCABULARY

Explain the difference between the following sets of words:

1. air pressure/altitude

2. troposphere/thermosphere

3. greenhouse effect/global warming

4. convection/conduction

5. global wind/local wind

6. primary pollutant/secondary pollutant

UNDERSTANDING CONCEPTS

Multiple Choice

7. What is the most abundant gas in the air that we breathe?
   a. oxygen   c. hydrogen
   b. nitrogen   d. carbon dioxide

8. The major source of oxygen for the Earth's atmosphere is
   a. sea water.   c. plants.
   b. the sun.   d. animals.

9. The bottom layer of the atmosphere, where almost all weather occurs, is the
   a. stratosphere.
   b. troposphere.
   c. thermosphere.
   d. mesosphere.

10. About ___?___ percent of the solar energy that reaches the outer atmosphere is absorbed at the Earth's surface.
    a. 20
    b. 30
    c. 50
    d. 70

11. The ozone layer is located in the
    a. stratosphere.
    b. troposphere.
    c. thermosphere.
    d. mesosphere.

12. How does most thermal energy in the atmosphere move?
    a. conduction
    b. convection
    c. advection
    d. radiation

13. The balance between incoming and outgoing energy is called ___?___.
    a. convection
    b. conduction
    c. greenhouse effect
    d. radiation balance

14. Most of the United States is located in which prevailing wind belt?
    a. westerlies
    b. northeast trade winds
    c. southeast trade winds
    d. doldrums

15. Which of the following is not a primary pollutant?
    a. car exhaust
    b. acid precipitation
    c. smoke from a factory
    d. fumes from burning plastic

16. The Clean Air Act
    a. controls the amount of air pollutants that can be released from most sources.
    b. requires cars to run on fuels other than gasoline.
    c. requires many industries to use scrubbers.
    d. (a) and (c) only

Short Answer

17. Why does the atmosphere become less dense as altitude increases?

18. Explain why air rises when it is heated.

19. What causes temperature changes in the atmosphere?

20. What are secondary pollutants, and how are they formed? Give an example.

Concept Mapping

21. Use the following terms to create a concept map: altitude, air pressure, temperature, atmosphere.

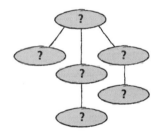

CRITICAL THINKING AND PROBLEM SOLVING

Write one or two sentences to answer the following questions:

22. What is the relationship between the greenhouse effect and global warming?

23. How do you think the Coriolis effect would change if the Earth were to rotate twice as fast? Explain.

24. Without the atmosphere, the Earth's surface would be very different. What are several ways that the atmosphere affects the Earth?

MATH IN SCIENCE

25. Wind speed is measured in miles per hour and in knots. One mile (statute mile or land mile) is 5,280 ft. One nautical mile (or sea mile) is 6,076 ft. Speed in nautical miles is measured in knots. Calculate the wind speed in knots if the wind is blowing at 25 mi/h.

INTERPRETING GRAPHICS

Use the wind-chill chart to answer the questions below.

Wind-Chill Chart						
		Actual thermometer reading (°F)				
Wind Speed		40	30	20	10	0
Knots	mph	Equivalent temperature (°F)				
Calm		40	30	20	10	0
4	5	37	27	16	6	−5
9	10	28	16	4	−9	−21
13	15	22	9	−5	−18	−36
17	20	18	4	−10	−25	−39
22	25	16	0	−15	−29	−44
26	30	13	−2	−18	−33	−48
30	35	11	−4	−20	−35	−49

26. If the wind speed is 20 mi/h and the temperature is 40°F, how cold will the air seem?

27. If the wind speed is 30 mi/h and the temperature is 20°F, how cold will the air seem?

Reading Check-up Take a minute to review your answers to the Pre-Reading Questions found at the bottom of page 2. Have your answers changed? If necessary, revise your answers based on what you have learned since you began this chapter.

Particles in the Air

Take a deep breath. You have probably just inhaled thousands of tiny specks of dust, pollen, and other particles. These particles, called particulates, are harmless under normal conditions. But if concentrations of particulates get too high or if they consist of harmful materials, they are considered to be a type of air pollution.

Because many particulates are very small, our bodies' natural filters, such as nasal hairs and mucous membranes, cannot filter all of them out. When inhaled, particulates can cause irritation in the lungs. Over time, this irritation can lead to diseases such as bronchitis, asthma, and emphysema. The danger increases as the level of particulates in the air increases.

▲ *When the ash from Mount St. Helens settled from the air, it created scenes like this one.*

Where There's Smoke . . .

Unfortunately, dust and pollen are not the only forms of particulates. Many of the particulates in the air come from the burning of various materials. For example, when wood is burned, it releases particles of smoke, soot, and ash into the air. Some of these are so small that they can float in the air for days. The burning of fuels such as coal, oil, and gasoline also creates particulates. The particulates from these sources can be very dangerous in high concentrations. That's why particulate concentrations are one measure of air quality. Large concentrations of particulates are visible in the air. Along with other pollutants, particulates are what make polluted air look brown or yellowish brown. But don't be fooled—even air that appears clean can be polluted.

Eruptions of Particulates

Volcanoes can be the source of incredible amounts of particulates. For example, when Mount St. Helens erupted in 1980, it launched thousands of tons of ash into the surrounding air. The air was so thick with ash that the area became as dark as night. For several hours, the ash completely blocked the light from the sun. When the ash finally settled from the air, it covered the surrounding landscape like a thick blanket of snow. This layer of ash killed plants and livestock for several kilometers around the volcano.

One theory to explain the extinction of dinosaurs is that a gargantuan meteorite hit the Earth with such velocity that the resulting impact created enough dust to block out the sun for years. During this dark period, plants were unable to grow and therefore could not support the normal food chains. Consequently, the dinosaurs died out.

Do Filters Really Filter?

▶ Since the burning of most substances creates particulates, there must be particulates in cigarette smoke. Do some research to find out if the filters on cigarettes are effective at preventing particulates from entering the smoker's body. Your findings may surprise you!

A Cure for Air Pollution?

Automobile emissions are responsible for at least half of all urban air pollution and a quarter of all carbon dioxide released into the atmosphere. Therefore, the production of a car that emits no polluting gases in its exhaust is a significant accomplishment. The only such vehicle currently available is the electric car. Electric cars are powered by batteries, so they do not produce exhaust gases. Supporters believe that switching to electric cars will reduce air pollution in this country. But critics believe that taxpayers will pay an unfair share for this switch and that the reduction in pollution won't be as great as promised.

▲ *Will a switch to electric cars such as this one reduce air pollution?*

Electric Cars Will Reduce Air Pollution

Even the cleanest and most modern cars emit pollutants into the air. Supporters of a switch to electric cars believe the switch will reduce pollution in congested cities. But some critics suggest that a switch to electric cars will simply move the source of pollution from a car's tailpipe to the power plant's smokestack. This is because most electricity is generated by burning coal.

In California, electric cars would have the greatest impact. Here most electricity is produced by burning natural gas, which releases less air pollution than burning coal.

Nuclear plants and dams release no pollutants in the air when they generate electricity. Solar power and wind power are also emission-free ways to generate electricity. Supporters argue that a switch to electric cars will reduce air pollution immediately and that a further reduction will occur when power plants convert to these cleaner sources of energy.

Electric Cars Won't Solve the Problem

Electric cars are inconvenient because the batteries have to be recharged so often. The batteries also have to be replaced every 2 to 3 years. The nation's landfills are already crowded with conventional car batteries, which contain acid and metals that may pollute ground water. A switch to electric cars would aggravate this pollution problem because the batteries have to be replaced so often.

Also, electric cars will likely replace the cleanest cars on the road, not the dirtiest. A new car may emit only one-tenth of the pollution emitted by an older model. If an older car's pollution-control equipment does not work properly, it may emit 100 times more pollution than a new car. But people who drive older, poorly maintained cars probably won't be able to afford expensive electric cars. Therefore, the worst offenders will stay on the road, continuing to pollute the air.

Analyze the Issue

▶ Do you think electric cars are the best solution to the air pollution problem? Why or why not? What are some alternative solutions for reducing air pollution?

Understanding Weather

Pre-Reading
Questions

1. Name some different
   kinds of clouds. How are
   they different?

2. What causes weather?

Twisting Terror

North America experiences an average of 700 tornadoes per year—more tornadoes than any other continent. Most of these tornadoes hit an area in the central United States called Tornado Alley. Tornado Alley has more tornadoes than any other area because its flatness and location on the Earth's surface make it possible for warm air masses and cold air masses to collide. In this chapter, you will learn about what causes weather and how weather can suddenly turn violent.

A MEETING OF THE MASSES

In this activity, you will model what happens when two air masses with different temperature characteristics meet.

Procedure

1. Fill a **beaker** with **500 mL of cooking oil.** Fill another **beaker** with **500 mL of water.** The cooking oil represents a less dense warm air mass. The water represents a denser cold air mass.

2. Predict what would happen if you tried to mix the two liquids together. Record your prediction in your ScienceLog.

3. Pour the contents of each beaker into a **clear, plastic rectangular container** at the same time from opposite ends of the container.

4. Observe what happens when the oil and water meet. Record your observations in your ScienceLog.

Analysis

5. What happens when the different liquids meet?

6. Does the prediction you made in step 2 match your results?

7. Based on your results, hypothesize what would happen if a cold air mass met a warm air mass. Record your hypothesis in your ScienceLog.

Terms to Learn

weather   condensation
water cycle   dew point
humidity   cloud
relative humidity   precipitation

What You'll Do

◆ Explain how water moves through the water cycle.

◆ Define *relative humidity.*

◆ Explain what the dew point is and its relation to condensation.

◆ Describe the three major cloud forms.

◆ Describe the four major types of precipitation.

Water in the Air

There might not be a pot of gold at the end of a rainbow, but rainbows hold another secret that you might not be aware of. Rainbows are evidence that the air contains water. Water droplets break up sunlight into the different colors that you can see in a rainbow. Water can exist in the air as a solid, liquid, or gas. Ice, a solid, is found in clouds as snowflakes. Liquid water exists in clouds as water droplets. And water in gaseous form exists in the air as water vapor. Water in the air affects the weather. **Weather** is the condition of the atmosphere at a particular time and place. In this section you will learn how water affects the weather.

The Water Cycle

Water in liquid, solid, and gaseous states is constantly being recycled through the water cycle. The **water cycle** is the continuous movement of water from water sources, such as lakes and oceans, into the air, onto and over land, into the ground, and back to the water sources. Look at **Figure 1** below to see how water moves through the water cycle.

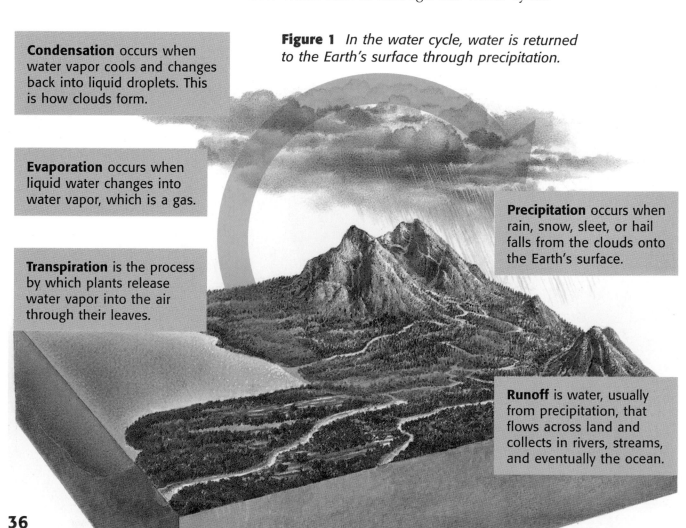

Condensation occurs when water vapor cools and changes back into liquid droplets. This is how clouds form.

Evaporation occurs when liquid water changes into water vapor, which is a gas.

Transpiration is the process by which plants release water vapor into the air through their leaves.

Figure 1 *In the water cycle, water is returned to the Earth's surface through precipitation.*

Precipitation occurs when rain, snow, sleet, or hail falls from the clouds onto the Earth's surface.

Runoff is water, usually from precipitation, that flows across land and collects in rivers, streams, and eventually the ocean.

Humidity

Have you ever spent a long time styling your hair before school and had a bad hair day anyway? You walked outside and—wham—your straight hair became limp, or your curly hair became frizzy. Most bad hair days can be blamed on humidity. **Humidity** is the amount of water vapor or moisture in the air. And it is the moisture in the air that makes your hair go crazy, as shown in **Figure 2.**

As water evaporates, the humidity of the air increases. But air's ability to hold water vapor depends on air temperature. As temperature increases, the air's ability to hold water also increases. **Figure 3** shows the relationship between air temperature and air's ability to hold water.

Figure 2 When there is more water in the air, your hair absorbs moisture and becomes longer.

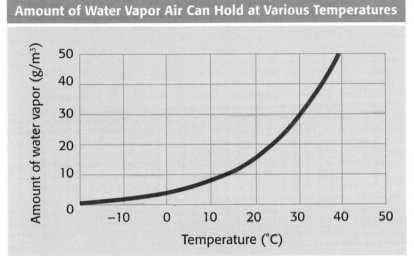

Amount of Water Vapor Air Can Hold at Various Temperatures

Figure 3 This graph shows that warmer air can hold more water vapor than cooler air.

Relative Humidity **Relative humidity** is the amount of moisture the air contains compared with the maximum amount it can hold at a particular temperature. Relative humidity is given as a percentage. When air holds all the water it can at a given temperature, the air is said to be *saturated*. Saturated air has a relative humidity of 100 percent. But how do you find the relative humidity of air that is not saturated? If you know the maximum amount of water vapor air can hold at a particular temperature and you know how much water vapor the air is actually holding, you can calculate the relative humidity.

Suppose that 1 m³ of air at a certain temperature can hold 24 g of water vapor. However, you know that the air actually contains 18 g of water vapor. You can calculate the relative humidity using the following formula:

$$\frac{\text{(present) } 18 \text{ g/m}^3}{\text{(saturated) } 24 \text{ g/m}^3} \times 100 = \text{(relative humidity) } 75\%$$

÷ ⁵ ÷ Ω ≤ ∞ +Ω √ 9 ∞ ≤ Σ 2
+

MATH BREAK

Relating Relative Humidity
Assume that a sample of air 1 m³ at 25°C, contains 11 g of water vapor. Calculate the relative humidity of the air using the value for saturated air shown in Figure 3.

Self-Check

How does humidity relate to the water cycle? *(Turn to page 136 to check your answer.)*

Water Vapor Versus Temperature If the temperature stays the same, relative humidity changes as water vapor enters or leaves the air. The more water vapor that is in the air at a particular temperature, the higher the relative humidity is. Relative humidity is also affected by changes in temperature. If the amount of water vapor in the air stays the same, the relative humidity decreases as the temperature rises and increases as the temperature drops.

Measuring Relative Humidity A *psychrometer* (sie KRAHM uht uhr) is an instrument used to measure relative humidity. It consists of two thermometers. One thermometer is called a wet-bulb thermometer. The bulb of this thermometer is covered with a damp cloth. The other thermometer is a dry-bulb thermometer. The dry-bulb thermometer measures air temperature.

As air passes over the wet-bulb thermometer, the water in the cloth begins to evaporate. As the water evaporates from the cloth, energy is transferred away from the wet-bulb and the thermometer begins to cool. If there is less humidity in the air, the water will evaporate more quickly and the temperature of the wet-bulb thermometer will drop. If the humidity is high, only a small amount of water will evaporate from the wet-bulb thermometer and there will be little change in temperature.

Follow the Numbers

Relative Humidity (in percentage)								
Dry-bulb reading (°C)	Difference between wet-bulb reading and dry-bulb reading (°C)							
	1	2	3	4	5	6	7	8
0	81	64	46	29	13			
2	84	68	52	37	22	7		
4	85	71	57	43	29	16		
6	86	73	60	48	35	24	11	
8	87	75	63	51	40	29	19	8
10	88	77	66	55	44	34	24	15
12	89	78	68	58	48	39	29	21
14	90	79	70	60	51	42	34	26
16	90	81	71	63	54	46	38	30
18	91	82	73	65	57	49	41	34
20	91	83	74	66	59	51	44	37

Relative humidity can be determined using a table such as this one. Locate the column that shows the difference between the wet-bulb and dry-bulb readings. Then locate the row that lists the temperature reading on the dry-bulb thermometer. The value where the column and row intersect is the relative humidity.

The difference in temperature readings between the wet-bulb and dry-bulb thermometers indicates the amount of water vapor in the air. A larger difference between the two readings indicates that there is less water vapor in the air and thus lower humidity.

The Process of Condensation

You have probably seen water droplets form on the outside of a glass of ice water, as shown in **Figure 4.** Did you ever wonder where those water droplets came from? The water came from the surrounding air, and droplets formed because of condensation. **Condensation** is the process by which a gas, such as water vapor, becomes a liquid. Before condensation can occur, the air must be saturated; it must have a relative humidity of 100 percent. Condensation occurs when saturated air cools further.

Figure 4 *Condensation occurred when the air next to the glass cooled to below its dew point.*

Dew Point Air can become saturated when water vapor is added to the air through evaporation or transpiration. Air can also become saturated, as in the case of the glass of ice water, when it cools to its dew point. The **dew point** is the temperature to which air must cool to be completely saturated. The ice in the glass of water causes the air surrounding the glass to cool to its dew point.

Before it can condense, water vapor must also have a surface to condense on. On the glass of ice water, water vapor condenses on the sides of the glass. Another example you may already be familiar with is water vapor condensing on grass, forming small water droplets called *dew.*

SECTION REVIEW

1. What is the difference between humidity and relative humidity?

2. What are two ways that air can become saturated with water vapor?

3. What does a relative humidity of 75 percent mean?

4. How does the water cycle contribute to condensation?

5. **Analyzing Relationships** What happens to relative humidity as the air temperature drops below the dew point?

Clouds

Some look like cotton balls, some look like locks of hair, and others look like blankets of gray blocking out the sun. But what *are* clouds and how do they form? And why are there so many different-looking clouds? A **cloud** is a collection of millions of tiny water droplets or ice crystals. Clouds form as warm air rises and cools. As the rising air cools, it becomes saturated. At saturation the water vapor changes to a liquid or a solid depending on the air temperature. At higher temperatures, water vapor condenses on small particles, such as dust, smoke, and salt, suspended in the air as tiny water droplets. At temperatures below freezing, water vapor changes directly to a solid, forming ice crystals.

Figure 5 *Cumulus clouds look like piles of cotton balls.*

Cumulus Clouds Puffy, white clouds that tend to have flat bottoms, as shown in **Figure 5,** are called *cumulus clouds.* Cumulus clouds form when warm air rises. These clouds generally indicate fair weather. However, when these clouds get larger they produce thunderstorms. A cumulus cloud that produces thunderstorms is called a *cumulonimbus cloud.* When *-nimbus* or *nimbo-* is part of a cloud's name, it means that precipitation might fall from the cloud.

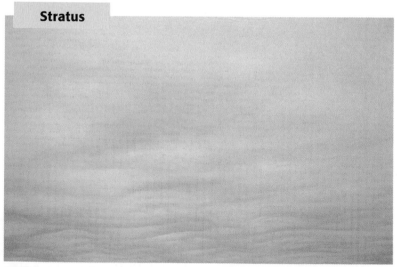

Figure 6 *Although stratus clouds are not as tall as cumulus clouds, they cover more area.*

Stratus Clouds Clouds that form in layers, as shown in **Figure 6,** are called *stratus clouds.* Stratus clouds cover large areas of the sky, often blocking out the sun. These clouds are caused by a gentle lifting of a large body of air into the atmosphere. *Nimbostratus clouds* are dark stratus clouds that usually produce light to heavy, continuous rain. When water vapor condenses near the ground, it forms a stratus cloud called *fog.*

Cirrus Clouds As you can see in **Figure 7,** *cirrus* (SIR uhs) *clouds* are thin, feathery, white clouds found at high altitudes. Cirrus clouds form when the wind is strong. Cirrus clouds may indicate approaching bad weather if they thicken and lower in altitude.

Clouds are also classified by the altitude at which they form. The illustration in **Figure 8** shows the three altitude groups used to categorize clouds.

Figure 7 *Cirrus clouds are made of ice crystals.*

Figure 8 Cloud Types Based on Form and Altitude

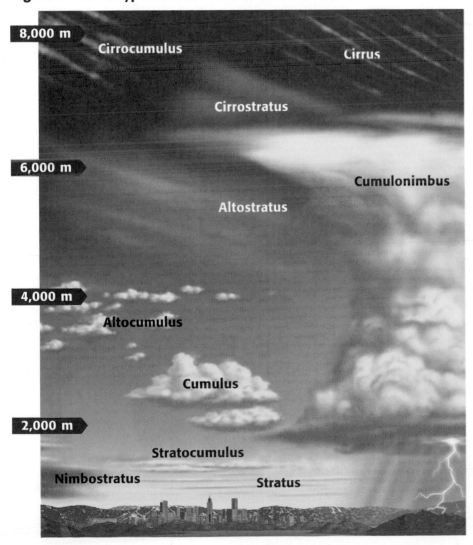

8,000 m

Cirrocumulus

Cirrus

Cirrostratus

6,000 m

Cumulonimbus

Altostratus

4,000 m

Altocumulus

Cumulus

2,000 m

Stratocumulus

Nimbostratus

Stratus

High Clouds
Because of the cold temperatures at high altitude, high clouds are made up of ice crystals. The prefix *cirro-* is used to describe high clouds.

Middle Clouds
Middle clouds can be made up of both water droplets and ice crystals. The prefix *alto-* is used to describe middle clouds.

Low Clouds
Low clouds are made up of water droplets. The prefix *strato-* is commonly used to describe these types of clouds.

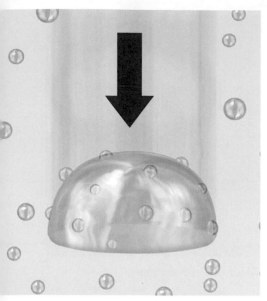

Figure 9 *Cloud droplets get larger by colliding and joining with other droplets. When the water droplets become too heavy, they fall as precipitation.*

Precipitation

Water vapor that condenses to form clouds can eventually fall to the ground as precipitation. **Precipitation** is water, in solid or liquid form, that falls from the air to the Earth. There are four major forms of precipitation—rain, snow, sleet, and hail.

Rain, the most common form of precipitation, is liquid water that falls from the clouds to Earth. A cloud produces rain when its water droplets become large enough to fall. A cloud droplet begins as a water droplet smaller than the period at the end of this sentence. Before a cloud droplet falls as precipitation, it must increase in size to about 100 times its normal diameter. **Figure 9** illustrates how a water droplet increases in size until it is finally large enough to fall as precipitation.

Snow and Sleet The most common form of solid precipitation is *snow.* Snow forms when temperatures are so cold that water vapor changes directly to a solid. Snow can fall as individual ice crystals or combine to form snowflakes, like the one shown in **Figure 10.**

Sleet, also called freezing rain, forms when rain falls through a layer of freezing air. The rain freezes, producing falling ice. Sometimes rain does not freeze until it hits a surface near the ground. When this happens, the rain changes into a layer of ice called *glaze,* as shown in **Figure 11.**

Figure 10 *Snowflakes are six-sided ice crystals that range in size from several millimeters to several centimeters.*

Figure 11 *Glaze ice forms as rain freezes on surfaces near the ground.*

Hail Solid precipitation that falls as balls or lumps of ice is called *hail*. Hail usually forms in cumulonimbus clouds. Updrafts of air in the clouds carry raindrops to high altitudes in the cloud, where they freeze. As the frozen raindrops fall, they collide and combine with water droplets. Another updraft of air can send the hail up again high into the cloud. Here the water drops collected by the hail freeze, forming another layer of frozen ice. If the upward movement of air is strong enough, the hail can accumulate many layers of ice. Eventually, the hail becomes too heavy and falls to the Earth's surface, as shown

Figure 12 *The impact of large hailstones can damage property and crops.*

in **Figure 12.** Hail is usually associated with warm weather and most often occurs during the spring and summer months.

Measuring Precipitation A *rain gauge* is an instrument used to measure the amount of rainfall. A rain gauge typically consists of a funnel and a cylinder, as shown in **Figure 13.** Rain falls into the funnel and collects in the cylinder. Markings on the cylinder indicate how much rain has fallen.

Snow is measured by both depth and water content. The depth of snow is measured using a measuring stick. The snow's water content is determined by melting the snow and measuring the amount of water.

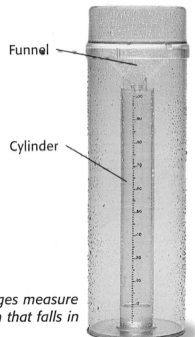

Funnel

Cylinder

Figure 13 *Rain gauges measure only the precipitation that falls in a particular place.*

SECTION REVIEW

1. How do clouds form?

2. Why are some clouds formed from water droplets, while others are made up of ice crystals?

3. Describe how rain forms.

4. **Applying Concepts** How can rain and hail fall from the same cumulonimbus cloud?

internet connect

*sci*LINKS.

NSTA

TOPIC: Collecting Weather Data
GO TO: www.scilinks.org
*sci*LINKS **NUMBER:** HSTE380

What You'll Do

◆ Explain how air masses are characterized.

◆ Describe the four major types of air masses that influence weather in the United States.

◆ Describe the four major types of fronts.

◆ Relate fronts to weather changes.

Air Masses and Fronts

Have you ever wondered how the weather can change so fast? One day the sun is shining and you are wearing shorts, and the next day it is so cold you need a coat. Changes in weather are caused by the movement and interaction of air masses. An **air mass** is a large body of air that has similar temperature and moisture throughout. In this section you will learn about air masses and how their interaction influences the weather.

Air Masses

An air mass gets its moisture and temperature characteristics from the area over which it forms. These areas are called *source regions*. For example, an air mass that develops over the Gulf of Mexico is warm and wet because this area is warm and has a lot of water that evaporates into the air. There are many types of air masses, each associated with a particular source region. The characteristics of these air masses are represented on maps with a two-letter symbol, as shown in **Figure 14.** The first letter indicates the moisture characteristics of the air mass, and the second symbol represents the temperature characteristics of the air mass.

Figure 14 *This map shows the source regions for air masses that influence weather in North America.*

maritime (m)–forms over water; wet

continental (c)–forms over land; dry

polar (P)–forms over the polar regions; cold

tropical (T)–develops over the Tropics; warm

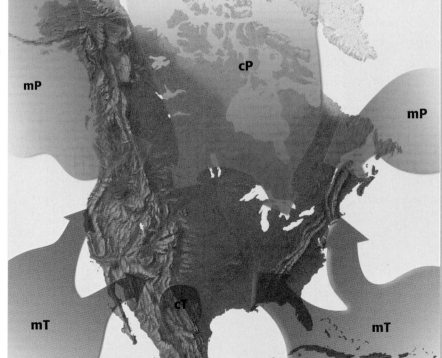

Cold Air Masses Most of the cold winter weather in the United States is influenced by three polar air masses. A continental polar air mass develops over land in northern Canada. In the winter, this air brings extremely cold weather to the United States, as shown in **Figure 15.** In the summer, it generally brings cool, dry weather.

A maritime polar air mass that forms over the North Pacific Ocean mostly affects the Pacific Coast. This air mass is very wet, but not as cold as the air mass that develops over Canada. In the winter, this air mass brings rain and snow to the Pacific Coast. In the summer, it brings cool, foggy weather.

Figure 15 *A cP air mass generally moves southeastward across Canada and into the northern United States.*

A maritime polar air mass that forms over the North Atlantic Ocean usually affects New England and eastern Canada. In the winter, it produces cold, cloudy weather with precipitation. In the summer, the air mass brings cool weather with fog.

Warm Air Masses Four warm air masses influence the weather in the United States. A maritime tropical air mass that develops over warm areas in the North Pacific Ocean is lower in moisture content and weaker than the maritime polar air mass. As a result, southern California receives less precipitation than the rest of California.

Other maritime tropical air masses develop over the warm waters of the Gulf of Mexico and the North Atlantic Ocean. These air masses move north across the East Coast and into the Midwest. In the summer, they bring hot and humid weather, thunderstorms, and hurricanes, as shown in **Figure 16.** In the winter, they bring mild, often cloudy weather.

Figure 16 *People in Texas experience the many thunderstorms brought by mT air masses from the Gulf of Mexico.*

A continental tropical air mass forms over the deserts of northern Mexico and the southwestern United States. This air mass influences weather in the United States only during the summer. It generally moves northeastward, bringing clear, dry, and very hot weather.

Fronts

Air masses with different characteristics, such as temperature and humidity, do not usually mix. So when two different air masses meet, a boundary forms between them. This boundary is called a **front.** Weather at a front is usually cloudy and stormy. The four different types of fronts—cold fronts, warm fronts, occluded fronts, and stationary fronts—are illustrated on these two pages. Fronts are usually associated with weather in the middle latitudes, where there are both cold and warm air masses. Fronts do not occur in the Tropics because only warm air masses exist there.

Cold Front

A cold air mass meets and displaces a warm air mass. Because the moving cold air is more dense, it moves under the less-dense warm air, pushing it up.

Cold fronts can move fast, producing thunderstorms, heavy rain, or snow. Cooler weather usually follows a cold front because the warm air is pushed away from the Earth's surface.

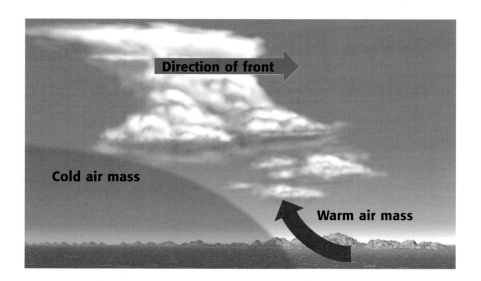

Warm Front

A warm air mass meets and overrides a cold air mass. The warm, less-dense air moves over the cold, denser air. The warm air gradually replaces the cold air.

Warm fronts generally bring drizzly precipitation. After the front passes, weather conditions are clear and warm.

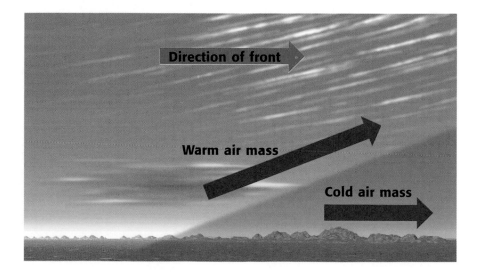

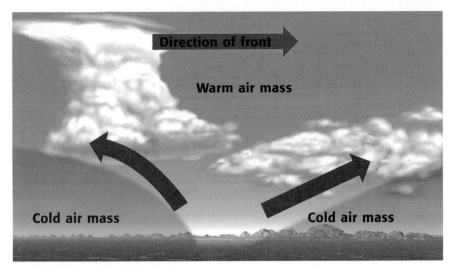

Direction of front

Warm air mass

Cold air mass

Cold air mass

Occluded Front

A faster-moving cold air mass overtakes a slower-moving warm air mass and forces the warm air up. The cold air mass then continues advancing until it meets a cold air mass that is warmer. The cold air mass then forces this air mass to rise.

An occluded front has cool temperatures and large amounts of precipitation.

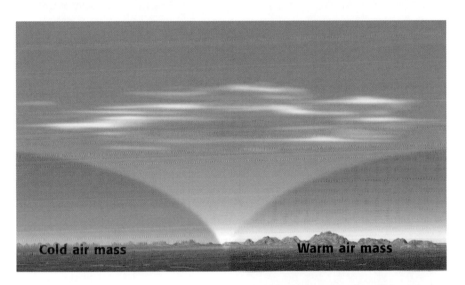

Cold air mass

Warm air mass

Stationary Front

A cold air mass meets a warm air mass and little horizontal movement occurs.

The weather associated with a stationary front is similar to that produced by a warm front.

SECTION REVIEW

1. What are the characteristics that define air masses?

2. What are the major air masses that influence the weather in the United States?

3. What are fronts, and what causes them?

4. What kind of front forms when a cold air mass displaces a warm air mass?

5. **Analyzing Relationships** Explain why the Pacific Coast has cool, wet winters and warm, dry summers.

internet**connect**

SC*L*INKS.
NSTA

TOPIC: Air Masses and Fronts
GO TO: www.scilinks.org
*sci*LINKS NUMBER: HSTE385

Terms to Learn

thunderstorm   tornado
lightning   hurricane
thunder

What You'll Do

◆ Explain what lightning is.
◆ Describe the formation of thunderstorms, tornadoes, and hurricanes.
◆ Describe the characteristics of thunderstorms, tornadoes, and hurricanes.

Severe Weather

Weather in the mid-latitudes can change from day to day. These changes result from the continual shifting of air masses. Sometimes a series of storms will develop along a front and bring severe weather. *Severe weather* is weather that can cause property damage and even death. Examples of severe weather include thunderstorms, tornadoes, and hurricanes. In this section you will learn about the different types of severe weather and how each type forms.

Thunderstorms

Thunderstorms, as shown in **Figure 17,** are small, intense weather systems that produce strong winds, heavy rain, lightning, and thunder. As you learned in the previous section, thunderstorms can occur along cold fronts. But that's not the only place they develop. There are only two atmospheric conditions required to produce thunderstorms: the air near the Earth's surface must be warm and moist, and the atmosphere must be unstable. The atmosphere is unstable when the surrounding air is colder than the rising air mass. As long as the air surrounding the rising air mass is colder, the air mass will continue to rise.

Thunderstorms occur when warm, moist air rises rapidly in an unstable atmosphere. When the warm air reaches its dew point, the water vapor in the air condenses, forming cumulus clouds. If the atmosphere is extremely unstable, the warm air will continue to rise, causing the cloud to grow into a dark, cumulonimbus cloud. These clouds can reach heights of more than 15 km.

Figure 17 *A typical thunderstorm produces approximately 470 million liters of water and enough electricity to provide power to the entire United States for 20 minutes.*

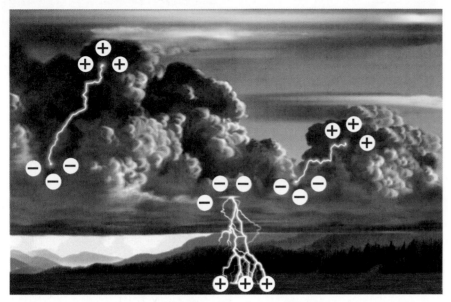

Figure 18 *The upper part of a cloud usually carries a positive electrical charge, while the lower part of the cloud carries mainly negative charges.*

Physics
CONNECTION

Have you ever wondered why you don't see lightning and hear thunder at the same time? Well, there's an easy explanation. Light travels faster than sound. The light reaches you almost instantly, but the sound travels only 1 km every 3 seconds. The closer the lightning is to where you are, the sooner you will hear the thunder.

Lightning Thunderstorms are very active electrically. **Lightning** is a large electrical discharge that occurs between two oppositely charged surfaces, as shown in **Figure 18.** Have you ever touched someone after scuffing your feet on the carpet and received a mild shock? If so, you have experienced how lightning forms. While walking around, friction between the floor and your shoes builds up an electrical charge in your body. When you touch someone else, the charge is released.

When lightning strikes, energy is released. This energy is transferred to the air and causes the air to expand rapidly and send out sound waves. **Thunder** is the sound that results from the rapid expansion of air along the lightning strike.

Severe Thunderstorms Severe thunderstorms produce one or more of the following conditions—high winds, hail, flash floods, and tornadoes. Hailstorms damage crops, dent the metal on cars, and break windows. Sudden flash flooding due to heavy rains causes millions of dollars in property damage annually and is the biggest cause of weather-related deaths.

Lightning, which occurs with all thunderstorms, is responsible for thousands of forest fires each year in the United States. Lightning also kills or injures hundreds of people a year in the United States.

Figure 19 *Lightning often strikes the highest object in an area.*

Tornadoes

Tornadoes are produced in only 1 percent of all thunderstorms. A **tornado** is a small, rotating column of air that has high wind speeds and low central pressure and that touches the ground. A tornado starts out as a funnel cloud that pokes through the bottom of a cumulonimbus cloud and hangs in the air. It is called a tornado when it makes contact with the Earth's surface. **Figure 20** shows the development of a tornado.

Figure 20 How a Tornado Forms

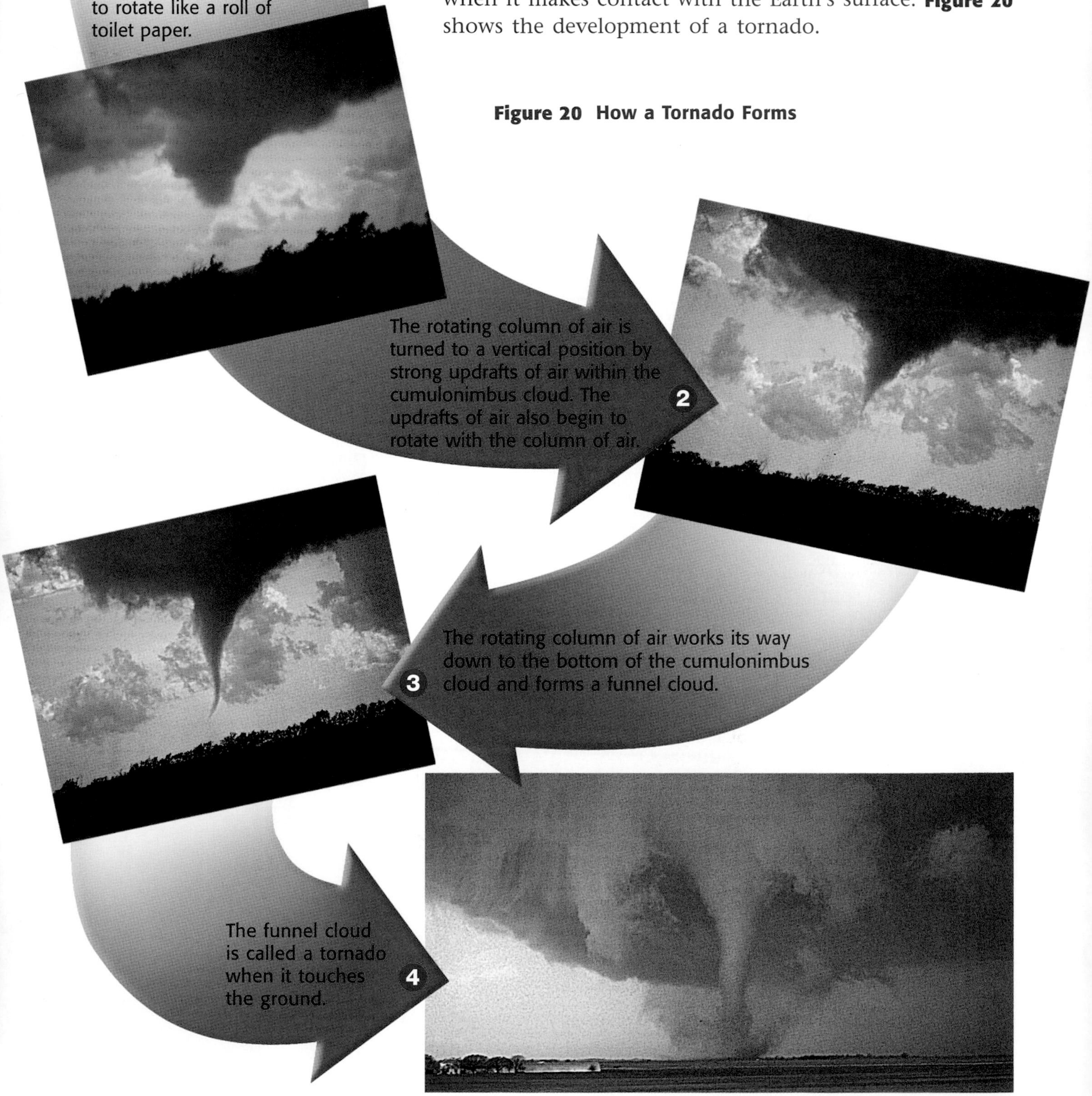

1 Wind traveling in two different directions causes a layer of air in the middle to begin to rotate like a roll of toilet paper.

The rotating column of air is turned to a vertical position by strong updrafts of air within the cumulonimbus cloud. The updrafts of air also begin to rotate with the column of air. **2**

The rotating column of air works its way down to the bottom of the cumulonimbus cloud and forms a funnel cloud. **3**

The funnel cloud is called a tornado when it touches the ground. **4**

Twists of Terror About 75 percent of the world's tornadoes occur in the United States. The majority of these tornadoes happen in the spring and early summer when cold, dry air from Canada collides with warm, moist air from the Tropics. The length of a tornado's path of destruction can vary, but it is usually about 8 km long and 10–60 m wide. Although most tornadoes last only a few minutes, they can cause a lot of damage. This is due to their strong spinning winds. The average tornado has wind speeds between 120 and 180 km/h, but rarer, more violent tornadoes can have spinning winds up to 500 km/h. The winds of tornadoes have been known to uproot trees and destroy buildings, as shown in **Figure 21.** Tornadoes are capable of picking up heavy objects, such as mobile homes and cars, and hurling them through the air.

Figure 21 *The tornado that hit Kissimmee, Florida, in 1998 had wind speeds of up to 416 km/h.*

Hurricanes

A **hurricane,** as shown in **Figure 22,** is a large, rotating tropical weather system with wind speeds of at least 119 km/h. Hurricanes are the most powerful storms on Earth. Hurricanes have different names in other parts of the world. In the western Pacific Ocean, they are called *typhoons.* Hurricanes that form over the Indian Ocean are called *cyclones.*

Hurricanes generally form in the area between 5° and 20° north and south latitude over warm, tropical oceans. At higher latitudes, the water is too cold for hurricanes to form. Hurricanes vary in size from 160 km to 1,500 km in diameter, and they can travel for thousands of miles.

BRAIN FOOD

Did you know that fish have been known to fall from the sky? Some scientists think the phenomenon of raining fish is caused by waterspouts. A waterspout is a tornado that occurs over water.

Figure 22 Hurricane Fran Photographed from Space

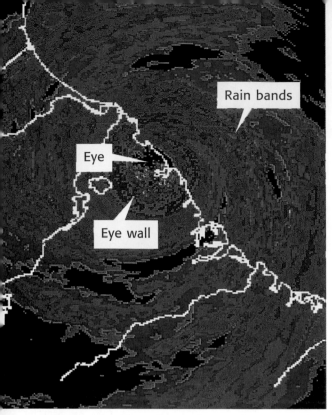

Rain bands

Eye

Eye wall

Figure 23 *The photo above gives you a bird's-eye view of a hurricane.*

Formation of a Hurricane A hurricane begins as a group of thunderstorms moving over tropical ocean waters. Winds traveling in two different directions collide, causing the storm to rotate over an area of low pressure. Because of the Coriolis effect, the storm turns counterclockwise in the Northern Hemisphere and clockwise in the Southern Hemisphere.

Hurricanes get their energy from the condensation of water vapor. Once formed, the hurricane is fueled through contact with the warm ocean water. Moisture is added to the warm air by evaporation from the ocean. As the warm, moist air rises, the water vapor condenses, releasing large amounts of energy. The hurricane continues to grow as long as it is over its source of warm, moist air. When the hurricane moves into colder waters or over land, it begins to die because it has lost its source of energy. **Figure 23** and **Figure 24** show two views of a hurricane.

Figure 24 *The view below shows how a hurricane would look if you cut it in half and looked at it from the side. The arrows indicate the flow of air.*

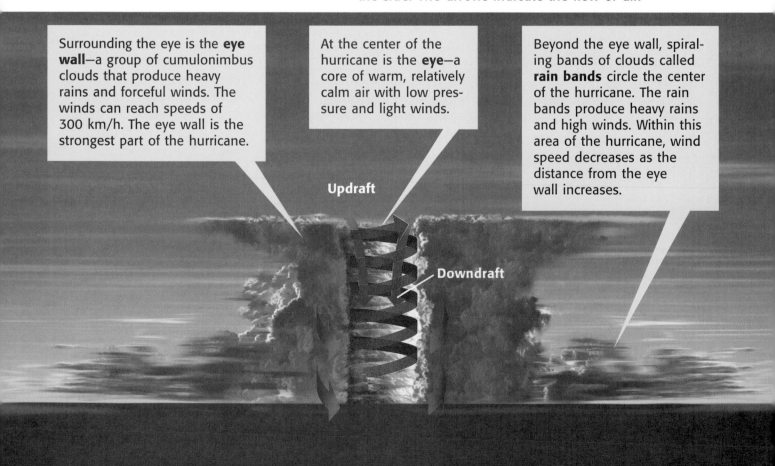

Surrounding the eye is the **eye wall**—a group of cumulonimbus clouds that produce heavy rains and forceful winds. The winds can reach speeds of 300 km/h. The eye wall is the strongest part of the hurricane.

At the center of the hurricane is the **eye**—a core of warm, relatively calm air with low pressure and light winds.

Beyond the eye wall, spiraling bands of clouds called **rain bands** circle the center of the hurricane. The rain bands produce heavy rains and high winds. Within this area of the hurricane, wind speed decreases as the distance from the eye wall increases.

Updraft

Downdraft

Damage Caused by Hurricanes Hurricanes can cause a lot of damage when they move near or onto land. The speed of the steady winds of most hurricanes ranges from 120 km/h to 150 km/h, and they can reach speeds as high as 300 km/h. Hurricane winds can knock down trees and telephone poles and can damage and destroy buildings and homes.

While high winds cause a great deal of damage, most hurricane damage is caused by flooding associated with heavy rains and storm surges. A *storm surge* is a wall of water that builds up over the ocean due to the heavy winds and low atmospheric pressure. The wall of water gets bigger and bigger as it nears the shore, reaching its greatest height when it crashes onto the shore. Depending on the hurricane's strength, a storm surge can be 1 m to 8 m high and 65 km–160 km long. Flooding causes tremendous damage to property and lives when a storm surge moves onto shore, as shown in **Figure 25.**

Astronomy
CONNECTION

The weather on Jupiter is more exciting than that on Earth. Wind speeds reach up to 540 km/h. Storms last for decades, and one—the Great Red Spot of Jupiter—has been swirling around since it was first discovered, in 1664. The Great Red Spot has a diameter of more than one and a half times that of the Earth. It is like a hurricane that has lasted more than 300 years.

Figure 25 *In 1998, the flooding associated with Hurricane Mitch devastated Central America. Whole villages were swept away by the flood waters and mudslides. Thousands of people were killed, and damages were estimated to be more than $5 billion.*

SECTION REVIEW

1. What is lightning?

2. Describe how tornadoes develop. What is the difference between a funnel cloud and a tornado?

3. Why do hurricanes form only over certain areas?

4. **Inferring Relationships** What happens to a hurricane as it moves over land? Why?

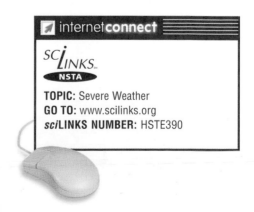

internet**connect**

SCiLINKS
NSTA

TOPIC: Severe Weather
GO TO: www.scilinks.org
*sci***LINKS NUMBER:** HSTE390

Terms to Learn

thermometer   wind vane
barometer   anemometer
windsock   isobars

What You'll Do

◆ Describe the different types of instruments used to take weather measurements.
◆ Explain how to interpret a weather map.
◆ Explain why weather maps are useful.

Forecasting the Weather

Have you ever left your house in the morning wearing a short-sleeved shirt, only to need a sweater in the afternoon? At some time in your life, you have been caught off guard by the weather. Weather affects how you dress and your daily plans, so it is important that you get accurate weather forecasts. A *weather forecast* is a prediction of weather conditions over the next 3 to 5 days. Meteorologists observe and collect data on current weather conditions in order to provide reliable predictions. In this section you will learn about some of the methods used to collect weather data and how those data are displayed.

Weather Forecasting Technology

In order for meteorologists to accurately forecast the weather, they need to measure various atmospheric conditions, such as air pressure, humidity, precipitation, temperature, wind speed, and wind direction. Meteorologists use special instruments to collect data on weather conditions both near and far above the Earth's surface. You have already learned about two tools that meteorologists use near the Earth's surface—psychrometers, which are used to measure relative humidity, and rain gauges, which are used to measure precipitation. Read on to learn about other methods meteorologists use to collect data.

Measuring Air Temperature A **thermometer** is a tool used to measure air temperature. A common type of thermometer uses a liquid sealed in a narrow glass tube, as shown in **Figure 26.** When air temperature increases, the liquid expands and moves up the glass tube. As air temperature decreases, the liquid shrinks and moves down the tube.

Air temperature is measured in both degrees Celsius and degrees Fahrenheit. In the United States, television weather forecasters generally report air temperature in degrees Fahrenheit.

Figure 26 *A liquid thermometer is usually filled with alcohol that is colored red, or mercury, which is silver.*

Measuring Air Pressure A **barometer** is an instrument used to measure air pressure. The mercurial barometer provides the most accurate method of measuring air pressure. A mercurial barometer consists of a glass tube sealed at one end that is placed in a container full of mercury. The air pressure pushes on the mercury inside the container, causing the mercury to move up the glass tube. The greater the air pressure is, the higher the mercury will rise.

Measuring Wind Direction Wind direction can be measured using a **windsock** or a **wind vane.** A windsock, as shown in **Figure 27,** is a cone-shaped cloth bag open at both ends. The wind enters through the wide end and leaves through the narrow end. Therefore, the wide end points into the wind.

A wind vane is shaped like an arrow with a large tail and is attached to a pole. The wind pushes the tail of the wind vane, spinning it on the pole until the arrow points into the wind.

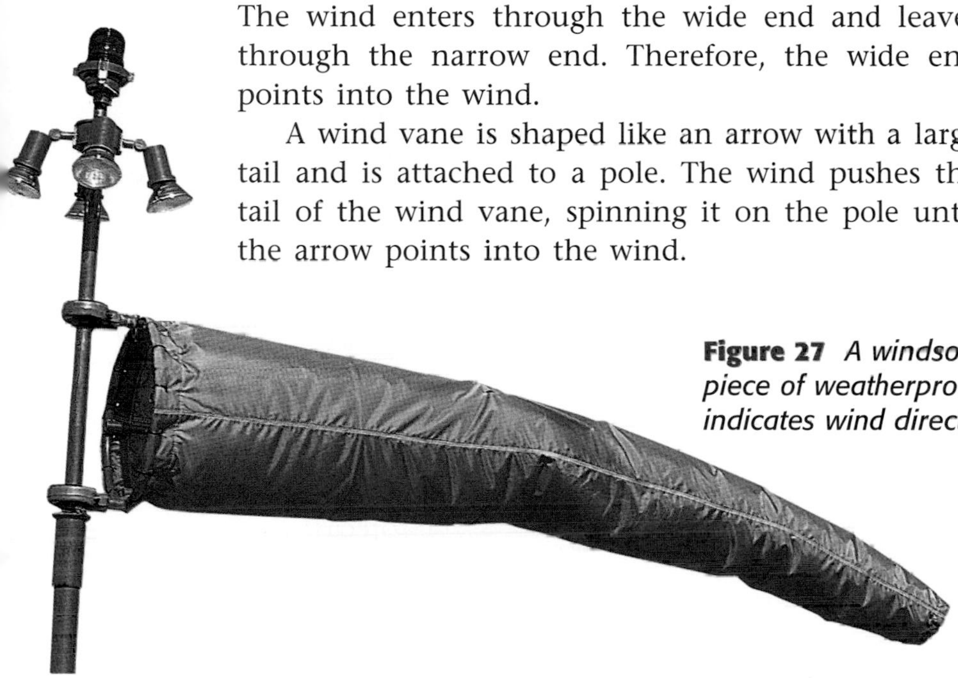

Figure 27 *A windsock is a cone-shaped piece of weatherproof material that indicates wind direction.*

Measuring Wind Speed Wind speed is measured by a device called an **anemometer.** An anemometer, as shown in **Figure 28,** consists of three or four cups connected by spokes to a pole. The wind pushes on the hollow sides of the cups, causing them to rotate on the pole. The motion sends a weak electrical current that is measured and displayed on a dial.

Measuring Weather in the Upper Atmosphere You have learned how weather conditions are recorded near the Earth's surface. But in order for meteorologists to better understand weather patterns, they must collect data from higher altitudes. Studying weather at higher altitudes requires the use of more-sophisticated equipment.

Figure 28 *The faster the wind speed is, the faster the cups of the anemometer spin.*

Figure 29 *Weather balloons carry radio transmitters that send measurements to stations on the ground.*

Eyes in the Sky Weather balloons carry electronic equipment that can measure weather conditions as high as 30 km above the Earth's surface. Weather balloons, such as the one in **Figure 29,** carry equipment that measures temperature, air pressure, and relative humidity.

Radar is used to find the location, movement, and intensity of precipitation. It can also detect what form of precipitation a weather system is carrying. You might be familiar with a type of radar called Doppler radar. **Figure 30** shows how Doppler radar is used to track precipitation.

Figure 30 *Using Doppler radar, meteorologists can predict a tornado up to 20 minutes before it touches the ground.*

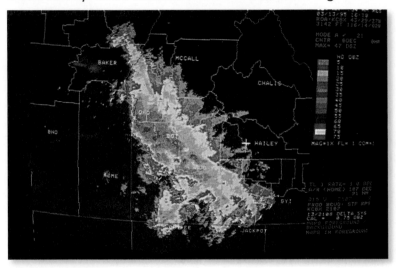

Activity

Throughout history, people have predicted approaching weather by interpreting natural signs. Animals and plants are usually more sensitive to changes in the atmosphere, such as air pressure, humidity, and temperature, than humans. To find out more about natural signs, research this topic at the library or on the Internet. Try searching using key words and phrases such as "weather and animals" or "weather and plants." Write a short paper on your findings to share with the class.

TRY at HOME

Weather satellites orbiting the Earth provide the images of the swirling clouds you can see on television weather reports. Satellites can measure wind speeds, humidity, and the temperatures at various altitudes.

Weather Maps

As you have learned, meteorologists base their forecasts on information gathered from many sources. In the United States, the National Weather Service (NWS) and the National Oceanic and Atmospheric Administration (NOAA) collect and analyze weather data. The NWS produces weather maps based on information gathered from about 1,000 weather stations across the United States. On these maps, each station is represented by a station model. A *station model*, as shown in **Figure 31,** is a small circle, which shows the location of the weather station, with a set of symbols and numbers surrounding it, which represent the weather data.

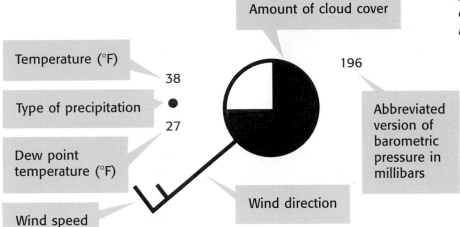

Temperature (°F)

Amount of cloud cover

Type of precipitation

Dew point temperature (°F)

Wind speed

Wind direction

38

27

196

Abbreviated version of barometric pressure in millibars

Figure 31 *Weather conditions at a station are represented by symbols.*

Under Pressure Weather maps also include lines called isobars. Isobars are similar to contour lines on a topographical map, except **isobars** are lines that connect points of equal air pressure rather than equal elevation. Isobar lines that form closed circles represent areas of high or low pressure. These areas are usually marked on a map with a capital *H* or *L*. Fronts are also labeled on weather maps. Weather maps, like the one shown in **Figure 32,** provide useful information for making accurate weather forecasts.

Figure 32 *Can you identify the different fronts on the weather map?*

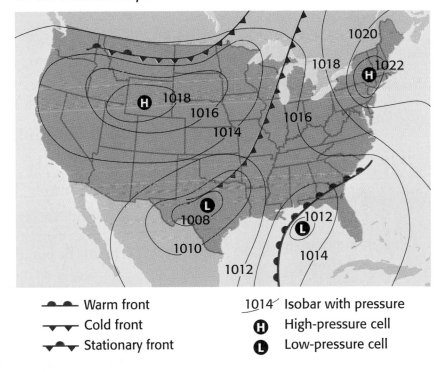

▲●▲● Warm front

▼▼▼ Cold front

▼●▼● Stationary front

1014 Isobar with pressure

H High-pressure cell

L Low-pressure cell

SECTION REVIEW

1. What are three methods meteorologists use to collect weather data?

2. What are weather maps based on?

3. What does a station model represent?

4. **Inferring Conclusions** Why would a meteorologist compare a new weather map with one 24 hours old?

internet**connect**

SCI**LINKS**

NSTA

TOPIC: Forcasting the Weather
GO TO: www.scilinks.org
*sci***LINKS NUMBER:** HSTE395

Design Your Own Lab

Gone with the Wind

Pilots at the Fly Away Airport need your help—fast! Last night, lightning destroyed the orange windsock. This windsock helped pilots measure which direction the wind was blowing. But now the windsock is gone with the wind, and an incoming airplane needs to land. The pilot must know which direction the wind is blowing and is counting on you to make a device that can measure wind direction.

MATERIALS

- paper plate
- drawing compass
- metric ruler
- protractor
- index card
- scissors
- stapler
- straight plastic straw
- sharpened pencil
- thumbtack or pushpin
- magnetic compass
- small rock

Ask a Question

1 How can I measure wind direction?

Conduct an Experiment

2 Find the center of the plate by tracing around its edge with a drawing compass. The pointed end of the compass should poke a small hole in the center of the plate.

3 Use a ruler to draw a line across the center of the plate.

4 Use a protractor to help you draw a second line through the center of the plate. This new line should be at a 90° angle to the line you drew in step 3.

5 Moving clockwise, label each line *N, E, S,* and *W.*

6 Use a protractor to help you draw two more lines through the center of the plate. These lines should be at a 45° angle to the lines you drew in steps 3 and 4.

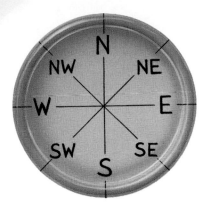

7 Moving clockwise from *N,* label these new lines *NE, SE, SW,* and *NW.* The plate now resembles the face of a magnetic compass. This will be the base of your wind-direction indicator. It will help you read the direction of the wind at a glance.

8 Measure and mark a 5 cm × 5 cm square on an index card. Cut the square out of the card. Fold the square in half to form a triangle.

9 Staple an open edge of the triangle to the straw so that one point of the triangle touches the end of the straw.

10 Hold the pencil at a 90° angle to the straw. The eraser should touch the balance point of the straw. Push a thumbtack or pushpin through the straw and into the eraser. The straw should spin without falling off.

11 Find a suitable area outside to measure the wind direction. The area should be clear of trees and buildings.

12 Press the sharpened end of the pencil through the center hole of the plate and into the ground. The labels on your paper plate should be facing the sky, as shown below.

13 Use a compass to find magnetic north. Rotate the plate so that the *N* on the plate points north. Place a small rock on top of the plate so that it does not turn.

14 You have just constructed a wind vane. Watch the straw as it rotates. The triangle will point in the direction the wind is blowing.

Analyze the Results

15 From which direction is the wind coming?

16 In which direction is the wind blowing?

Draw Conclusions

17 Would this be an effective way for pilots to measure wind direction? Why or why not?

18 What improvements would you suggest to Fly Away Airport to measure wind direction more accurately?

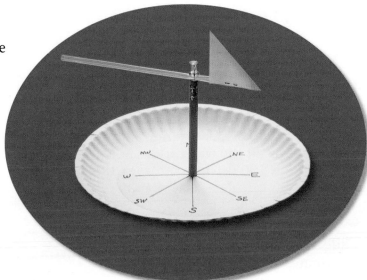

Chapter Highlights

SECTION 1

Vocabulary

weather *(p. 36)*

water cycle *(p. 36)*

humidity *(p. 37)*

relative humidity *(p. 37)*

condensation *(p. 39)*

dew point *(p. 39)*

cloud *(p. 40)*

precipitation *(p. 42)*

Section Notes

- Water is continuously moving and changing state as it moves through the water cycle.

- Humidity is the amount of water vapor or moisture in the air. Relative humidity is the amount of moisture the air contains compared with the maximum amount it can hold at a particular temperature.

- Water droplets form because of condensation.

- Dew point is the temperature to which air must cool to be saturated.

- Condensation occurs when the air next to a surface cools to below its dew point.

- Clouds are formed from condensation on dust and other particles above the ground.

- There are three major cloud forms—cumulus, stratus, and cirrus.

- There are four major forms of precipitation—rain, snow, sleet, and hail.

Labs

Let It Snow! *(p. 107)*

SECTION 2

Vocabulary

air mass *(p. 44)*

front *(p. 46)*

Section Notes

- Air masses form over source regions. An air mass has similar temperature and moisture content throughout.

- Four major types of air masses influence weather in the United States—maritime polar, maritime tropical, continental polar, continental tropical.

- A front is a boundary between contrasting air masses.

- There are four types of fronts—cold fronts, warm fronts, occluded fronts, and stationary fronts.

- Specific types of weather are associated with each front.

☑ Skills Check

Math Concepts

RELATIVE HUMIDITY Relative humidity is the amount of moisture the air is holding compared with the amount it can hold at a particular temperature. The relative humidity of air that is holding all the water it can at a given temperature is 100 percent, meaning it is saturated. You can calculate relative humidity with the following equation:

$$\frac{\text{(present) g/m}^3}{\text{(saturated) g/m}^3} \times 100 = \text{relative humidity}$$

Visual Understanding

HURRICANE HORSEPOWER Hurricanes are the most powerful storms on Earth. A cross-sectional view helps you identify the different parts of a hurricane. The diagram on page 52 shows a side view of a hurricane.

SECTION 3

Vocabulary

thunderstorm (*p. 48*)

lightning (*p. 49*)

thunder (*p. 49*)

tornado (*p. 50*)

hurricane (*p. 51*)

Section Notes

- Severe weather is weather that can cause property damage and even death.

- Thunderstorms are small, intense storm systems that produce lightning, thunder, strong winds, and heavy rain.

- Lightning is a large electrical discharge that occurs between two oppositely charged surfaces.

- Thunder is the sound that results from the expansion of air along a lightning strike.

- A tornado is a rotating funnel cloud that touches the ground.

- Hurricanes are large, rotating, tropical weather systems that form over the tropical oceans.

SECTION 4

Vocabulary

thermometer (*p. 54*)

barometer (*p. 55*)

windsock (*p. 55*)

wind vane (*p. 55*)

anemometer (*p. 55*)

isobars (*p. 57*)

Section Notes

- Weather balloons, radar, and weather satellites take weather measurements at high altitudes.

- Meteorologists present weather data gathered from stations as station models on weather maps.

Labs

Watching the Weather (*p. 104*)

---

internetconnect

GO TO: go.hrw.com

Visit the **HRW** Web site for a variety of learning tools related to this chapter. Just type in the keyword:

KEYWORD: HSTWEA

GO TO: www.scilinks.org

Visit the **National Science Teachers Association** on-line Web site for Internet resources related to this chapter. Just type in the *sci*LINKS number for more information about the topic:

TOPIC: Collecting Weather Data		*sci***LINKS NUMBER:** HSTE380	
TOPIC: Air Masses and Fronts		*sci***LINKS NUMBER:** HSTE385	
TOPIC: Severe Weather		*sci***LINKS NUMBER:** HSTE390	
TOPIC: Forecasting the Weather		*sci***LINKS NUMBER:** HSTE395	

Chapter Review

Explain the difference between the following sets of words:

1. relative humidity/dew point

2. condensation/precipitation

3. air mass/front

4. lightning/thunder

5. tornado/hurricane

6. barometer/anemometer

UNDERSTANDING CONCEPTS

Multiple Choice

7. The process of liquid water changing to gas is called
   a. precipitation.
   b. condensation.
   c. evaporation.
   d. water vapor.

8. What is the relative humidity of air at its dew-point temperature?
   a. 0 percent
   b. 50 percent
   c. 75 percent
   d. 100 percent

9. Which of the following is not a type of condensation?
   a. fog
   b. cloud
   c. snow
   d. dew

10. High clouds made of ice crystals are called __?__ clouds.
    a. stratus   c. nimbostratus
    b. cumulus   d. cirrus

11. Large thunderhead clouds that produce precipitation are called __?__ clouds.
    a. nimbostratus   c. cumulus
    b. cumulonimbus   d. stratus

12. Strong updrafts within a thunderhead can produce
    a. snow.   c. sleet.
    b. rain.   d. hail.

13. A maritime tropical air mass contains
    a. warm, wet air.   c. warm, dry air.
    b. cold, moist air. d. cold, dry air.

14. A front that forms when a warm air mass is trapped between cold air masses and forced to rise is called a(n)
    a. stationary front. c. occluded front.
    b. warm front.   d. cold front.

15. A severe storm that forms as a rapidly rotating funnel cloud is called a
    a. hurricane.   c. typhoon.
    b. tornado.   d. thunderstorm.

16. The lines on a weather map connecting points of equal atmospheric pressure are called
    a. contour lines.   c. isobars.
    b. highs.   d. lows.

Short Answer

17. Explain the relationship between condensation and the dew point.

18. Describe the conditions along a stationary front.

19. What are the characteristics of an air mass that forms over the Gulf of Mexico?

20. Explain how a hurricane develops.

Concept Mapping

21. Use the following terms to create a concept map: evaporation, relative humidity, water vapor, dew, psychrometer, clouds, fog.

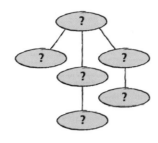

CRITICAL THINKING AND PROBLEM SOLVING

Write one or two sentences to answer the following questions:

22. If both the air temperature and the amount of water vapor in the air change, is it possible for the relative humidity to stay the same? Explain.

23. What can you assume about the amount of water vapor in the air if there is no difference between the wet- and dry-bulb readings of a psychrometer?

24. List the major similarities and differences between hurricanes and tornadoes.

MATH IN SCIENCE

You always see lightning before you hear thunder. That's because light travels at about 300,000,000 m/s, while sound travels only 330 m/s. One way you can determine how close you are to the thunderstorm is by counting how many seconds there are between the lightning and thunder. Usually, it takes thunder about 3 seconds to cover 1 km. Answer the following questions based on this estimate.

25. If you hear thunder 12 seconds after you see the flash of lightning, how far away is the thunderstorm?

26. If you hear thunder 36 seconds after you see the flash of lightning, how far away is the thunderstorm?

INTERPRETING GRAPHICS

Use the weather map below to answer the questions that follow.

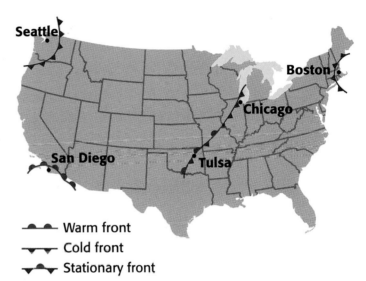

▲—▲— Warm front
▼▼— Cold front
▼—▲▼— Stationary front

27. Where are thunderstorms most likely to occur? Explain your answer.

28. What are the weather conditions like in Tulsa, Oklahoma? Explain your answer.

Reading Check-up

Take a minute to review your answers to the Pre-Reading Questions found at the bottom of page 84. Have your answers changed? If necessary, revise your answers based on what you have learned since you began this chapter.

CAREERS

METEOROLOGIST

Predicting floods, observing a tornado develop inside a storm, watching the growth of a hurricane, and issuing flood warnings are all in a day's work for **Cristy Mitchell.** As a meteorologist for the National Weather Service, Mitchell spends each working day observing the powerful forces of nature.

In addition to using computers, Mitchell also uses radar and satellite imagery to show regional and national weather. Meteorologists also use computerized models of the world's atmosphere to help forecast the weather.

Find Out for Yourself

▶ Use the library or the Internet to find information about hurricanes, tornadoes, or thunderstorms. How do meteorologists define these storms? What trends in air pressure, temperature, and humidity do meteorologists use to forecast storms?

When asked what made her job interesting, Mitchell replied, "There's nothing like the adrenaline rush you get when you see a tornado coming! I would say that witnessing the powerful forces of nature is what really makes my job interesting."

Meteorology is the study of natural forces in Earth's atmosphere. Perhaps the most familiar field of meteorology is weather forecasting. However, meteorology is also used in air-pollution control, agricultural planning, and air and sea transportation, and criminal and civil investigations. Meteorologists also study trends in Earth's climate, such as global warming and ozone depletion.

Collecting the Data

Meteorologists collect data on air pressure, temperature, humidity, and wind velocity. By applying what they know about the physical properties of the atmosphere and analyzing the mathematical relationships in the data, they are able to forecast the weather.

Meteorologists use a variety of tools, such as computers and satellites, to collect the data they need to make accurate weather forecasts. Mitchell explained, "The computer is an invaluable tool for me. Through it, I receive maps and detailed information, including temperature, wind speed, air pressure, lightning activity, and general sky conditions for a specific region."

▲ *This photograph of Hurricane Elena was taken from the space shuttle* Discovery *in September 1985.*

Science Fiction

"All Summer in a Day"

by Ray Bradbury

It is raining, just like it has been for 7 long years. That is 2,555 days of nonstop rain. For the men, women, and children who came to build a civilization on Venus, constant rain is a fact of life. But there is one special day—a day when it stops raining and the sun shines gloriously. This day comes about only once every 7 years. And today is that day!

At school the students have been looking forward to this day for weeks. In one class they've read about how the sun is like a lemon, and how hot it is. They've written stories and poems about what it might be like to see the sun.

And now that the day has finally arrived, all of the children in that class are peering through the window, searching for the sun. The children are 9 years old, and all of them but Margot have lived on Venus all their lives. None of them remember the day 7 years ago when the rain stopped. They only recall stories about the sunshine, and now they just can't wait to see it for themselves!

But Margot is different. She longs to see the sun even more than the others. The reason makes the other kids jealous. And jealous kids can be cruel. . . .

What happens to Margot? Find out for yourself by reading Ray Bradbury's "All Summer in a Day" in the *Holt Anthology of Science Fiction*.

Climate

Pre-Reading Questions

1. What is the difference between weather and climate?

2. List ways in which human influences such as pollution and technology can affect climate.

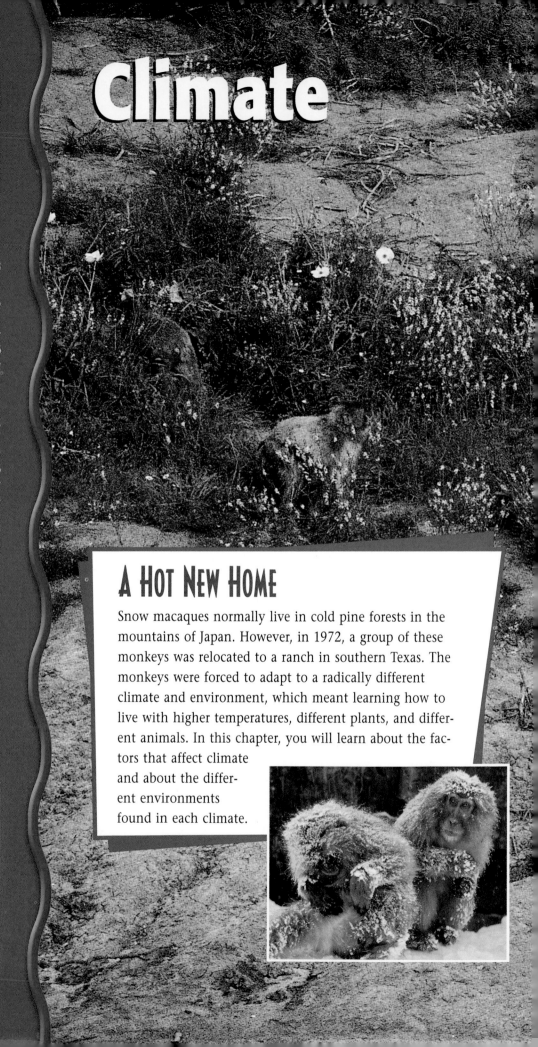

A Hot New Home

Snow macaques normally live in cold pine forests in the mountains of Japan. However, in 1972, a group of these monkeys was relocated to a ranch in southern Texas. The monkeys were forced to adapt to a radically different climate and environment, which meant learning how to live with higher temperatures, different plants, and different animals. In this chapter, you will learn about the factors that affect climate and about the different environments found in each climate.

WHAT'S YOUR ANGLE?

Because the Earth is round, the sun's solar rays strike the Earth's surface at different angles. Try this activity to find out how the amount of solar energy received at the equator differs from the amount received at the poles.

Procedure

1. Plug in a **lamp,** and position it 30 cm from a **globe.**

2. Point the lamp so that the light shines directly on the globe's equator.

3. Using **adhesive putty,** attach a **thermometer** to the globe's equator in a vertical position. Attach **another thermometer** to the globe's north pole so that the tip points toward the lamp.

4. Record the temperature reading of each thermometer in your ScienceLog.

5. Turn on the lamp, and let the light shine on the globe for 3 minutes.

6. When the time is up, turn off the lamp, and record the temperature reading of each thermometer again.

Analysis

7. Was there a difference between the final temperature at the globe's north pole and that at the globe's equator? If so, what was it?

Terms to Learn

weather	prevailing winds
climate	elevation
latitude	surface currents

What You'll Do

◆ Explain the difference between weather and climate.
◆ Identify the factors that determine climates.

What Is Climate?

You have just received a call from a friend who is coming to visit you tomorrow. He is wondering what clothing to bring and wants to know about the current weather in your area. You step outside, check to see if there are rain clouds in the sky, and note the temperature. But what if your friend asked you about the climate in your area? What is the difference between weather and climate?

The main difference between weather and climate has to do with time. **Weather** is the condition of the atmosphere at a particular time and place. Weather conditions vary from day to day. **Climate,** on the other hand, is the average weather conditions in an area over a long period of time. Climate is determined by two main factors, temperature and precipitation. Study the map in **Figure 1,** and see if you can describe the climate in northern Africa.

Figure 1 *How does the climate in northern Africa differ from the climate where you live?*

As you can see in **Figure 2,** if you were to take a trip around the world, or even across the United States, you would experience different climates. For example, if you visited the Texas coast in the summer, you would find it hot and humid. But if you visited interior Alaska during the summer, it would probably be much cooler and less humid. Why are the climates so different? The answer is complicated. It includes factors such as latitude, wind patterns, geography, and ocean currents.

Figure 2 *Summer in Texas is different from summer in Alaska.*

Latitude

Think of the last time you looked at a globe. Do you recall the thin horizontal lines that circle the globe? These horizontal lines are called lines of latitude. **Latitude** is the distance north or south, measured in degrees, from the equator. In general, the temperature of an area depends on its latitude. The higher the latitude is, the colder the climate is. For example, one of the coldest places on Earth, the North Pole, is at 90° north of the equator. On the other hand, the equator, which has a latitude of 0°, is hot.

It's Hot! It's Not! Why are there such temperature differences at different latitudes? The answer has to do with solar energy. Solar energy heats the Earth. Latitude determines the amount of solar energy a particular area receives. You can see how this works in **Figure 3.** Notice that the sun's rays hit the area around the equator directly, at nearly a 90° angle. At this angle, a small area of the Earth's surface receives more direct solar energy, resulting in high temperatures. Near the poles, however, the sun's rays strike the surface at a lesser angle than at the equator. This lesser angle spreads the same amount of solar energy over a larger area, resulting in lower temperatures.

Figure 3 *The sun's rays strike the Earth's surface at different angles because the surface is curved.*

Seasons and Latitude In most places in the United States, the year consists of four seasons. Winter is probably cooler than summer where you live. But there are places in the world that do not have such seasonal changes. For example, areas near the equator have approximately the same temperatures and same amount of daylight year-round. **Figure 4** shows how latitude determines the seasons.

Winter

During our winter months the Southern Hemisphere has higher temperatures and longer days because it tilts toward the sun and receives more direct solar energy. The Northern Hemisphere has lower temperatures and shorter days because it tilts away from the sun.

March 21

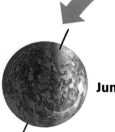

June 21

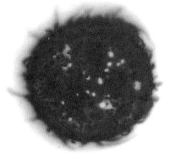

December 21

September 22

Summer

During our summer months the Northern Hemisphere has warmer temperatures and longer days because it tilts toward the sun and receives more direct solar energy for a longer amount of time. However, the Southern Hemisphere has colder temperatures and shorter days because it is tilted away from the sun.

Figure 4 *The Earth is tilted on its axis at a 23.5° angle. This tilt affects how much solar energy an area receives as the Earth moves around the sun.*

✓ Self-Check

During what months does Australia have summer? *(See page 136 to check your answer.)*

Prevailing Winds

Prevailing winds are winds that blow mainly from one direction. These winds influence an area's moisture and temperature. Before you learn how the prevailing winds affect climate, take a look at **Figure 5** to learn about some of the basic properties of air.

Figure 5 *Because warm air is less dense, it tends to rise. Cooler, denser air tends to sink.*

Cold air sinks, and as it sinks it warms.

When cold air is heated, it gains the ability to hold water vapor.

When warm air cools, it loses the ability to hold water vapor. This results in *precipitation.*

Warm air rises, and as it rises it cools.

Prevailing winds affect the amount of precipitation that a region receives. If the prevailing winds form from warm air, they will carry moisture. If the prevailing winds form from cold air, they will probably be dry.

The amount of moisture in prevailing winds is also affected by whether the winds blow across land or across a large body of water. Winds that travel across large bodies of water absorb moisture. Winds that travel across land tend to be dry. Even if a region borders the ocean, the area might be dry if the prevailing winds blow across the land, as shown in **Figure 6.**

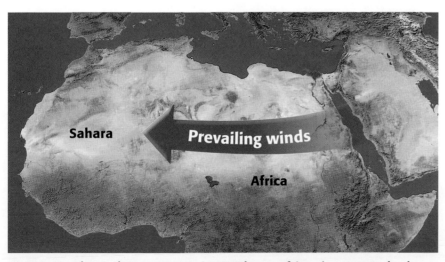

Figure 6 *The Sahara Desert, in northern Africa, is extremely dry because of the dry prevailing winds that blow across the continent.*

Quick Lab

A Cool Breeze

1. Hold a **thermometer** next to the top edge of a **cup of water** containing **two ice cubes.** Read the temperature next to the cup.

2. Have your lab partner fan the surface of the cup with a **paper fan.** Read the temperature again. Has the temperature changed? Why? Record your answer in your ScienceLog.

TRY at HOME

Activity

Using a physical map, locate the mountain ranges in the United States. Does climate vary from one side of a mountain range to the other? If so, what does this tell you about the climatic conditions on either side of the mountain? From what direction are the prevailing winds blowing?

TRY at HOME

Geography

Mountains can influence an area's climate by affecting both temperature and precipitation. For example, Kilimanjaro, the tallest mountain in Africa, has snow-covered peaks year-round, even though it is only about 3° (320 km) south of the equator. Temperatures on Kilimanjaro and in other mountainous areas are affected by elevation. **Elevation** is the height of surface landforms above sea level. As the elevation increases, the atmosphere becomes less dense. When the atmosphere is less dense, its ability to absorb and hold thermal energy is reduced and temperatures are therefore lower.

Mountains also affect the climate of nearby areas by influencing the distribution of precipitation. **Figure 7** shows how the climates on two sides of a mountain can be very different.

Figure 7 *Mountains block the prevailing winds from blowing across a continent, changing the amount of moisture the wind carries.*

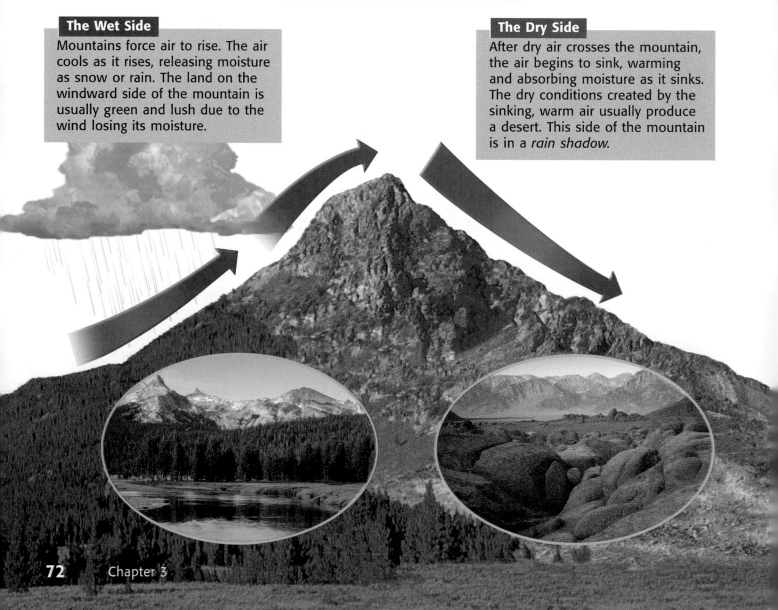

The Wet Side

Mountains force air to rise. The air cools as it rises, releasing moisture as snow or rain. The land on the windward side of the mountain is usually green and lush due to the wind losing its moisture.

The Dry Side

After dry air crosses the mountain, the air begins to sink, warming and absorbing moisture as it sinks. The dry conditions created by the sinking, warm air usually produce a desert. This side of the mountain is in a *rain shadow*.

Ocean Currents

Because of water's ability to absorb and release thermal energy, the circulation of ocean surface currents has an enormous effect on an area's climate. **Surface currents,** which can be either warm or cold, are streamlike movements of water that occur at or near the surface of the ocean. **Figure 8** shows the pattern of the major warm and cold ocean surface currents.

Current Events As surface currents move, they carry warm or cool water to different locations. The surface temperature of the water affects the temperature of the air above it. Warm currents heat the surrounding air and cause warmer temperatures, while cool currents cool the surrounding air and cause cooler temperatures. For example, the Gulf Stream current carries warm water northward off the east coast of North America past Iceland, an island country located just below the Arctic Circle. The warm water from the Gulf Stream heats the surrounding air, creating warmer temperatures in southern Iceland. Iceland experiences milder temperatures than Greenland, its neighboring island, where the climate is not influenced by the Gulf Stream.

Science CONNECTION

What is El Niño? Can it affect our health? Turn to page 94 to find out.

Figure 8 *The red arrows represent the movement of warm surface currents. The blue arrows represent the movement of cold surface currents.*

SECTION REVIEW

1. What is the difference between weather and climate?

2. How do mountains affect climate?

3. Describe how air temperature is affected by ocean surface currents.

4. **Analyzing Relationships** How would seasons be different if the Earth did not tilt on its axis?

internetconnect

SC*i*LINKS
NSTA

TOPIC: What Is Climate?
GO TO: www.scilinks.org
*sci*LINKS NUMBER: HSTE405

Climates of the World

Terms to Learn

biome   evergreens
tropical zone   polar zone
temperate zone   microclimate
deciduous

What You'll Do

◆ Locate and describe the three major climate zones.
◆ Describe the different biomes found in each climate zone.

Have you ever wondered why the types of plants and animals in one part of the world are different from those found in another part? One reason involves climate. Plants and animals that have adapted to one climate may not be able to live in another climate. For instance, frogs do not live in Antarctica.

The three major climate zones of Earth—tropical, temperate, and polar—are illustrated in **Figure 9.** Each zone has a temperature range that relates to its latitude. However, in each of these zones there are several types of climates due to differences in the geography and the amount of precipitation. Because of the various climates in each zone, there are different biomes. A **biome** is a large region characterized by a specific type of climate and the plants and animals that live there.

Figure 10 shows the distribution of the Earth's land biomes. In this section we will review each of the three major climate zones and the biomes that are found in each zone.

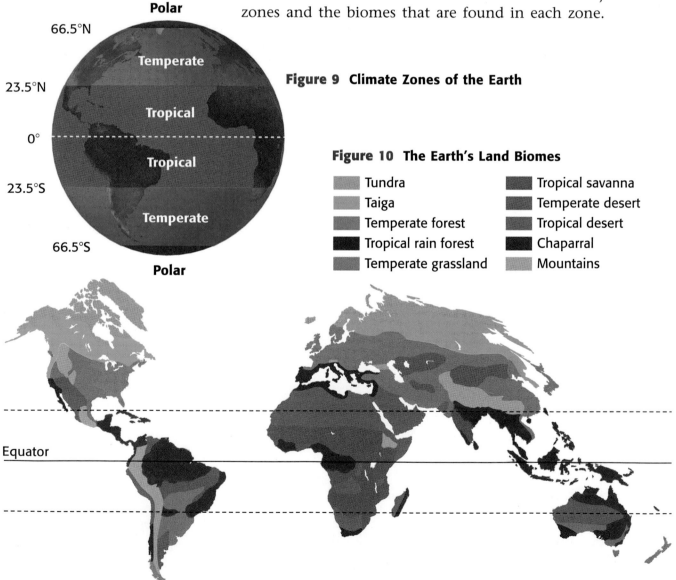

Figure 9 Climate Zones of the Earth

Figure 10 The Earth's Land Biomes

- Tundra
- Taiga
- Temperate forest
- Tropical rain forest
- Temperate grassland
- Tropical savanna
- Temperate desert
- Tropical desert
- Chaparral
- Mountains

The Tropical Zone

The **tropical zone,** or the *Tropics,* is the warm zone located around the equator, as shown in **Figure 11.** This zone extends from the tropic of Cancer to the tropic of Capricorn. As you have learned, latitudes in this zone receive the most solar radiation. Temperatures are therefore usually hot, except at high elevations. Within the tropical zone there are three types of biomes—tropical rain forest, tropical desert, and tropical savanna. **Figure 12** shows the distribution of these biomes.

Figure 11 The Earth's Tropical Zone

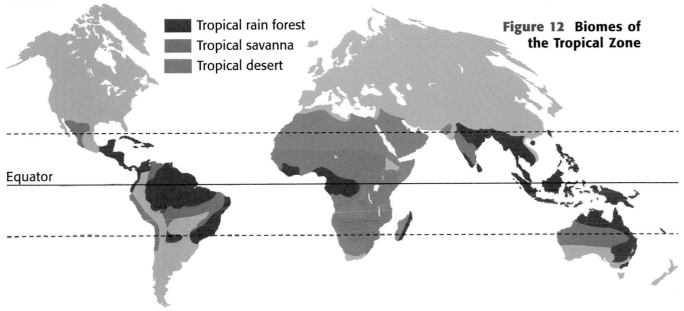

23.5°N

0°

23.5°S

- Tropical rain forest
- Tropical savanna
- Tropical desert

Equator

Figure 12 Biomes of the Tropical Zone

Tropical Rain Forest Tropical rain forests are always warm and wet. Because they are located near the equator, they receive strong sunlight year-round, causing little difference between seasons.

Tropical rain forests contain the greatest number of plant and animal species of any biome. But in spite of the lush vegetation, shown in **Figure 13,** the soil in rain forests is poor. The rapid decay of plants and animals returns nutrients to the soil, but these nutrients are quickly absorbed and used by the plants. The nutrients that are not immediately used by the plants are washed away by the heavy rains, leaving soil that is thin and nutrient poor.

Figure 13 *In tropical rain forests, many of the trees form aboveground roots that provide extra support for the trees in the thin soil.*

Avg. Temperature Range: 25°C–28°C (77°F–82°F)

Avg. Yearly Precipitation: 200 cm or more

Soil Characteristics: thin and nutrient poor

Vegetation: mahogany, ebony, rosewood, and balsa trees; vines, ferns, and bamboo

Animals: monkeys, lemurs, parrots, snakes, tree frogs, bats, pigs, small antelopes, tigers, jaguars, and leopards

Tropical Deserts A desert is an area that receives less than 25 cm of rainfall per year. Because of this low yearly rainfall, deserts are the driest places on Earth. Desert plants, shown in **Figure 14,** are adapted to survive in a place with little water.

Deserts can be divided into hot deserts and cold deserts. The majority of hot deserts, such as the Sahara, in Africa, are tropical deserts. Hot deserts are caused by cool sinking air masses. Daily temperatures in tropical deserts vary from very hot daytime temperatures (50°C) to cool nighttime temperatures (20°C). Winters in hot deserts are usually mild. Because of the dryness, the soil is poor in organic matter, which fertilizes the soil. The dryness makes it hard to break down dead organic matter.

Avg. Temperature Range: 16°C–50°C (61°F–120°F)

Avg. Yearly Precipitation: 0–25 cm

Soil Characteristics: poor in organic matter

Vegetation: succulents (cactus and euphorbia), shrubs, thorny trees

Animals: kangaroo rats, lizards, scorpions, snakes, birds, bats, toads

Some desert animals, such as the spadefoot toad, survive the scorching summer heat by burying themselves in the ground and sleeping through the dry season.

Figure 14 *Plants called succulents have adapted to dry conditions by developing fleshy stems and leaves to store water and a waxy coating to prevent water loss. A cactus is a type of succulent.*

Self-Check

If desert soil is so nutrient rich, why are deserts not suitable for agriculture? *(See page 136 to check your answer.)*

Tropical Savannas Tropical savannas, sometimes referred to as grasslands, are dominated by tall grasses, with trees scattered here and there. **Figure 15** is a photo of an African savanna. The climate is usually very warm, with a dry season that lasts four to eight months followed by short periods of rain. Savanna soils are generally nutrient poor, but grass fires, which are common during the dry season, leave the soils nutrient enriched.

Many plants have adapted to fire and use it to reproduce. Grasses sprout from their roots after the upper part of the plant is burned. The seeds of some plant species require fire in order to grow. For example, some species need fire to break open the seed's outer skin. Only after this skin is broken can the seed grow. Other species drop their seeds at the end of fire season. The heat from the fire triggers the plants to drop their seeds into the newly enriched soil.

Avg. Temperature Range: 27°C–32°C (80°F–90°F)

Avg. Yearly Precipitation: 100 cm

Soil Characteristics: generally nutrient poor

Vegetation: tall grasses (3–5 m), trees, thorny shrubs

Animals: gazelles, rhinoceroses, giraffes, lions, hyenas, ostriches, crocodiles, elephants

Figure 15 *The grass of a tropical savanna is 3–5 m tall, much taller than that of a temperate grassland.*

SECTION REVIEW

1. What are the soil characteristics of a tropical rain forest?

2. In what way has savanna vegetation adapted to fire?

3. **Summarizing Data** How do each of the tropical biomes differ?

internet**connect**

SC*LINKS*
NSTA

TOPIC: Climates of the World
GO TO: www.scilinks.org
*sci*LINKS NUMBER: HSTE410

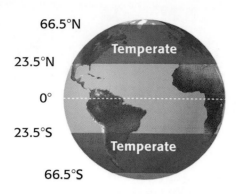

66.5°N

Temperate

23.5°N

0°

23.5°S

Temperate

66.5°S

Figure 16 The Earth's Temperate Zones

The Temperate Zone

The **temperate zone,** as shown in **Figure 16,** is the climate zone between the Tropics and the polar zone. Temperatures in the temperate zone tend to be moderate. The continental United States is in the temperate zone, which includes the following four biomes: temperate forest, temperate grassland, chaparral, and temperate desert. **Figure 17** shows the distribution of the biomes found in the temperate zone.

Figure 17 Biomes of the Temperate Zone

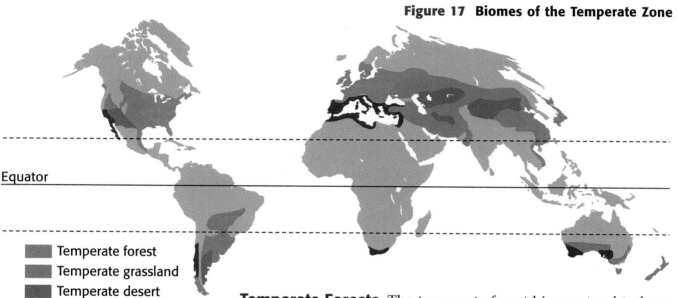

Equator

- Temperate forest
- Temperate grassland
- Temperate desert
- Chaparral

Temperate Forests The temperate forest biomes tend to have very high amounts of rainfall and seasonal temperature differences. Because of these distinct seasonal changes, summers are usually warm and winters are usually cold. The largest temperate forests are deciduous, such as the one shown in **Figure 18.** **Deciduous** trees are trees that lose their leaves when the weather becomes cold. These trees tend to be broad-leaved. The soils in deciduous forests are usually quite fertile because of the high organic content contributed by decaying leaves that drop every winter.

Figure 18 *Deciduous trees have leaves that change color and drop when temperatures become cold.*

Avg. Temperature Range: 0°C–28°C (32°F–82°F)

Avg. Yearly Precipitation: 76–250 cm

Soil Characteristics: very fertile, organically rich

Vegetation: deciduous and evergreen trees, shrubs, herbs

Animals: deer, bears, boars, badgers, squirrels, wolves, wild cats, red foxes, owls, and many other birds

Another type of temperate forest is the evergreen forest. **Evergreens** are trees that keep their leaves year-round. Evergreens can be either broad-leaved trees or needle-leaved trees, such as pine trees. Mixed forests of broad-leaved and needle-leaved trees can be found in humid climates, such as Florida, where winter temperatures rarely fall below freezing.

Temperate Grasslands Temperate grasslands, such as those shown in **Figure 19,** occur in regions that receive too little rainfall for trees to grow. This biome has warm summers and cold winters. The temperate grasslands are known by many local names—the *prairies* of North America, the *steppes* of Eurasia, the *veldt* of Africa, and the *pampas* of South America. Grasses are the most common type of vegetation found in this biome. Because grasslands have the most fertile soils of all biomes, much of the temperate grassland has been plowed to make room for croplands.

Avg. Temperature Range: −6°C–26°C (21°F–78°F)

Avg. Yearly Precipitation: 38–76 cm

Soil Characteristics: most fertile soils of all biomes

Vegetation: grasses

Animals: large grazing animals, including the bison of North America, the kangaroo of Australia, and the antelope of Africa

Figure 19 *The world's grasslands once covered about 42 percent of Earth's total land surface. Today they occupy only about 12 percent of the Earth's surface.*

Chaparrals Chaparral regions, as shown in **Figure 20,** have cool, wet winters and hot, dry summers. The vegetation is mainly evergreen shrubs, which are short, woody plants with thick, waxy leaves. The waxy leaves are adaptations that help prevent water loss in dry conditions. These shrubs grow in rocky, nutrient-poor soil. Like tropical-savanna vegetation, chaparral vegetation has adapted to fire. In fact, some plants, such as chamise, can grow back from their roots after a fire.

Avg. Temperature Range: 11°C–26°C (51°F–78°F)

Avg. Yearly Precipitation: 48–56 cm

Soil Characteristics: rocky, nutrient-poor soils

Vegetation: evergreen shrubs, scrubby trees, herbs

Animals: ground squirrels, deer, elk, mountain lions, coyotes, wolves

Figure 20 *Some plant species found in chaparral produce substances that help them catch on fire. These species require fire to reproduce.*

Temperate Deserts The temperate desert biomes, like the one shown in **Figure 21,** tend to be cold deserts. Like all deserts, cold deserts receive less than 25 cm of rainfall annually. Temperate deserts can be very hot in the daytime, but—unlike hot deserts—they tend to be very cold at night.

Avg. Temperature Range:
1°C–50°C (34°F–120°F)

Avg. Yearly Precipitation:
0–25 cm

Soil Characteristics: poor in organic matter

Vegetation: succulents (cactus), shrubs, thorny trees

Animals: kangaroo rats, lizards, scorpions, snakes, birds, bats, toads

Figure 21 *The Great Basin Desert is in the rain shadow of the Sierra Nevada.*

The temperatures sometimes drop below freezing. This large change in temperature between day and night is caused by low humidity and cloudless skies. These conditions allow for a large amount of energy to reach, and thus heat, the Earth's surface during the day. However, these same characteristics allow the energy to escape at night, causing temperatures to drop. You probably rarely think of snow and deserts together, but temperate deserts often receive light snow during the winter.

Temperate deserts are dry because they are generally located inland, far away from a moisture source, or are located on the rain-shadow side of a mountain range.

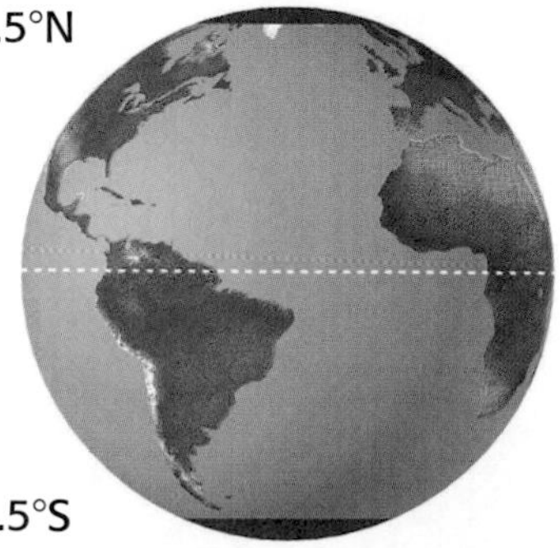

The Polar Zone

The **polar zone** includes the northernmost and southernmost climate zones, as shown in **Figure 22.** Polar climates have the coldest average temperatures. The temperatures in the winter stay below freezing, and the temperatures during the summer months remain chilly. **Figure 23,** on the next page, shows the distribution of the biomes found in the polar zone.

Polar

66.5°N

0°

66.5°S

Polar

Figure 22 The Earth's Polar Zones

Figure 23 Biomes of the Polar Zone

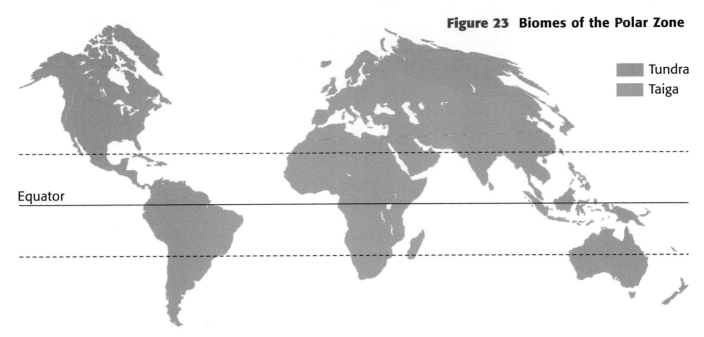

Tundra
Taiga

Equator

Tundra Next to deserts, the tundra, as shown in **Figure 24,** is the driest place on Earth. This biome has long, cold winters with almost 24 hours of night and short, cool summers with almost 24 hours of daylight. In the summer, only the top meter of soil thaws. Underneath the thawed soil lies a permanently frozen layer of soil, called *permafrost*. This frozen layer prevents the water in the thawed soil from draining. Because of the poor drainage, the upper soil layer is muddy and is therefore an excellent breeding ground for insects, such as mosquitoes. Many birds migrate to the tundra during the summer to feed on the insects.

Environment

C O N N E C T I O N

Subfreezing climates contain almost no decomposing bacteria. The well-preserved body of John Torrington, a member of an expedition that explored the Northwest Passage in Canada in the 1840s, was uncovered in 1984, appearing much as it did when he died, more than 140 years earlier.

Avg. Temperature Range:
–27°C–5°C (–17°F–41°F)

Avg. Yearly Precipitation:
0–25 cm

Soil Characteristics: frozen

Vegetation: mosses, lichens, sedges, and dwarf trees

Animals: rabbits, lemmings, reindeer, caribou, musk oxen, wolves, foxes, birds, and polar bears

Figure 24 *In the tundra, mosses and lichens cover rocks. Dwarf trees grow close to the ground to protect themselves from strong winds and to absorb energy from the Earth's sunlit surface.*

Climate   **81**

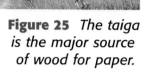

Figure 25 *The taiga is the major source of wood for paper.*

Taiga (Northern Coniferous Forest)

Just south of the tundra lies the taiga biome. The taiga, as shown in **Figure 25,** has long, cold winters and short, warm summers. Like the tundra, the soil during the winter is frozen. The majority of the trees are evergreen needle-leaved trees called *conifers,* such as pine, spruce, and fir trees. The needles and bendable branches allow these trees to shed heavy snow before they can be damaged. Conifer needles contain acidic substances. When the needles die and fall to the soil, they make the soil acidic. Most plants cannot grow in acidic soil, and therefore the forest floor is bare except for some mosses and lichens.

Avg. Temperature Range:
–10°C–15°C (14°F–59°F)

Avg. Yearly Precipitation:
40–61 cm

Soil Characteristics: acidic soil

Vegetation: mosses, lichens, conifers

Animals: birds, rabbits, moose, elk, wolves, lynxes, and bears

Microclimates

You have learned the types of biomes that are found in each climate zone. But the climate and the biome of a particular place can also be influenced by local conditions. **Microclimates** are small regions with unique climatic characteristics. For example, elevation can affect an area's climate and therefore its biome. Tundra and taiga biomes exist in the Tropics on high mountains. How is this possible? Remember that as the elevation increases, the atmosphere loses its ability to absorb and hold thermal energy. This results in lower temperatures.

Cities are also microclimates. In a city, temperatures can be 1°C to 2°C warmer than the surrounding rural areas. This is because buildings and pavement made of dark materials absorb solar radiation instead of reflecting it. There is also less vegetation to take in the sun's rays. This absorption of the sun's rays by buildings and pavement heats the surrounding air and causes temperatures to rise.

Physics CONNECTION

Roof temperatures can get so hot that you can fry an egg on them! In a study of roofs on a sunny day when the air temperature was 13°C, scientists recorded roof temperatures ranging from 18°C to 61°C depending on color and material of the roof.

To find out more about microclimates, turn to page 109 of the LabBook.

SECTION REVIEW

1. Describe how tropical deserts and temperate deserts differ.

2. List and describe the three major climate zones.

3. **Inferring Conclusions** Rank each biome according to how suitable it would be for growing crops. Explain your reasoning.

Terms to Learn

ice age
global warming
greenhouse effect

What You'll Do

◆ Describe how the Earth's climate has changed over time.
◆ Summarize the different theories that attempt to explain why the Earth's climate has changed.
◆ Explain the greenhouse effect and its role in global warming.

Changes in Climate

As you know, the weather constantly changes—sometimes several times in one day. Saturday, your morning baseball game was canceled because of rain, but by that afternoon the sun was shining. Now think about the climate where you live. You probably haven't noticed a change in climate, because climates change slowly. What causes climates to change? Until recently, climatic changes were connected only to natural causes. However, studies indicate that human activities may have an influence on climatic change. In this section, you will learn how natural and human factors may influence climatic change.

Ice Ages

The geologic record indicates that the Earth's climate has been much colder than it is today. In fact, much of the Earth was covered by sheets of ice during certain periods. An **ice age** is a period during which ice collects in high latitudes and moves toward lower latitudes. Scientists have found evidence of many major ice ages throughout the Earth's geologic history. The most recent ice age began about 2 million years ago.

Glacial Periods During an ice age, there are periods of cold and periods of warmth. These periods are called glacial and interglacial periods. During *glacial periods*, the enormous sheets of ice advance, getting bigger and covering a larger area as shown in **Figure 26.** Because a large amount of ocean water is frozen during glacial periods, sea level drops.

Figure 26 *During the last glacial period, which ended 10,000 years ago, the Great Lakes were covered by an enormous block of ice that was 1.5 km high.*

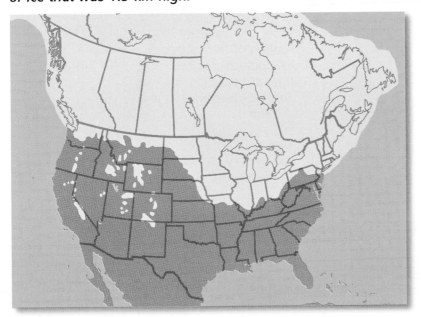

Interglacial Periods Warmer times that occur between glacial periods are called *interglacial periods*. During an interglacial period, the ice begins to melt and the sea level rises again. The last interglacial period began 10,000 years ago and is still occurring. Why do these periods occur? Will the Earth have another glacial period in the future? These questions have been debated by scientists for the past 200 years.

Motions of the Earth There are many theories about the causes of ice ages. Each theory attempts to explain the gradual cooling that leads to the development of enormous ice sheets that periodically cover large areas of the Earth's surface. The *Milankovitch theory* explains why an ice age isn't just one long cold spell but instead alternates between cold and warm periods. Milutin Milankovitch, a Yugoslavian scientist, proposed that changes in the Earth's orbit and in the tilt of the Earth's axis cause ice ages, as illustrated in **Figure 27.**

Figure 27 *According to the Milankovitch theory, the amount of solar radiation the Earth receives varies due to three kinds of changes in the Earth's orbit.*

① Over a period of 100,000 years, the Earth's orbit slowly changes from a more circular shape to a more elliptical shape. When the orbit is more elliptical, summers are hotter and winters are cooler. When the orbit is more circular, there is not as much seasonal change.

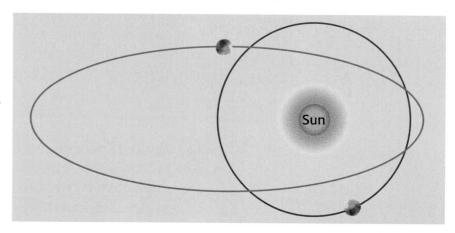

② Over a period of 41,000 years, the tilt of the Earth's axis varies between 21.8° and 24.4°. When the tilt is at 24.4°, the poles receive more solar energy.

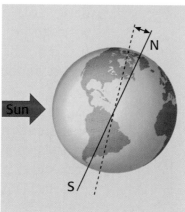

③ The Earth's axis traces a complete circle every 26,000 years. The circular motion of the Earth's axis determines the time of year that the Earth is closest to the sun.

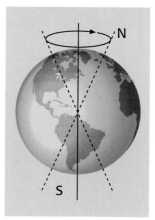

Self-Check

How do you think the Earth's elliptical orbit affects the amount of solar radiation that reaches the surface? *(See page 136 to check your answer.)*

Volcanic Eruptions There are many natural factors that can affect global climate. Catastrophic events, such as volcanic eruptions, can influence climate. Volcanic eruptions send large amounts of dust, ash, and smoke into the atmosphere. Once in the atmosphere, the dust, smoke, and ash particles act as a shield, blocking out so much of the sun's rays that the Earth cools. **Figure 28** shows how dust particles from a volcanic eruption block the sun.

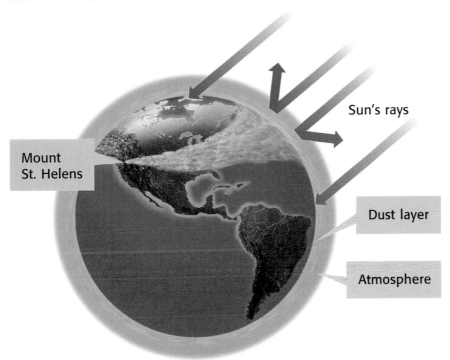

Sun's rays

Mount St. Helens

Dust layer

Atmosphere

Figure 28 *Volcanic eruptions, such as the one that occurred at Mount St. Helens, shown above, produce dust that reflects sunlight, as shown at left.*

Plate Tectonics The Earth's climate is further influenced by plate tectonics and continental drift. One theory proposes that ice ages occur when the continents are positioned closer to the polar regions. For example, approximately 250 million years ago, all the continents were connected near the South Pole in one giant landmass called Pangaea, as shown in **Figure 29.** During this time, ice covered a large area of the Earth's surface. As Pangaea broke apart, the continents moved toward the equator, and the ice age ended. During the last ice age, many large landmasses were positioned in the polar zones. Antarctica, northern North America, Europe, and Asia all were covered with large sheets of ice.

Pangaea

Figure 29 *Much of Pangaea—the part that is now Africa, South America, India, Antarctica, Australia, and Saudi Arabia—was covered by continental ice sheets.*

MATH BREAK

The Ride to School

Find out how much carbon dioxide is released into the atmosphere each month from the car or bus that transports you to school.

1. Figure out the distance from your home to school.

2. From this figure, calculate how many kilometers you travel to and from school, in a car or bus, per month.

3. Divide this number by 20. This represents approximately how many gallons of gas are used during your trips to school.

4. If burning 1 gal of gasoline produces 9 kg of carbon dioxide, how much carbon dioxide is released?

Global Warming

Is the Earth really experiencing global warming? **Global warming** is a rise in average global temperatures that can result from an increase in the greenhouse effect. To understand how global warming works, you must first learn about the greenhouse effect.

Greenhouse Effect   The **greenhouse effect** is the Earth's natural heating process, in which gases in the atmosphere trap thermal energy. The Earth's atmosphere performs the same function as the glass windows in a car. Think about the car illustrated in **Figure 30.** It's a hot summer day, and you are about to get inside the car. You immediately notice that it feels hotter inside the car than outside. Then you sit down and—ouch!—you burn yourself on the seat.

Figure 30 *Sunlight streams into the car through the clear glass windows. The seats absorb the radiant energy and change it into thermal energy. The energy is then trapped in the car.*

Window to the World   Greenhouse gases allow sunlight to pass through the atmosphere. It is absorbed by the Earth's surface and reradiated as thermal energy. Many scientists hypothesize that the rise in global temperatures is due to an increase of carbon dioxide, a greenhouse gas, as a result of human activity. Most evidence indicates that the increase in carbon dioxide is caused by the burning of fossil fuels that releases carbon dioxide into the atmosphere.

Another factor that may add to global warming is deforestation. *Deforestation* is the process of clearing forests, as shown in **Figure 31.** In many countries around the world, forests are being burned to clear land for agriculture. All types of burning release carbon dioxide into the atmosphere, thereby increasing the greenhouse effect. Plants use carbon dioxide to make food. As plants are removed from the Earth, the carbon dioxide that would have been used by the plants builds up in the atmosphere.

Figure 31 *Clearing land by burning leads to increased levels of carbon dioxide in the atmosphere.*

Consequences of Global Warming Many scientists think that if the average global temperature continues to rise, some regions of the world might experience flooding. Warmer temperatures could cause the icecaps to melt, raising the sea level and flooding low-lying areas, such as the coasts.

Areas that receive little rainfall, such as deserts, might receive even less due to increased evaporation. Scientists predict that the Midwest, an agricultural area, could experience warmer, drier conditions. A change in climate such as this could harm crops. But farther north, such as in Canada, weather conditions for farming would improve.

Reducing Pollution

A city just received a warning from the Environmental Protection Agency for exceeding the automobile fuel emissions standards. If you were the city manager, what suggestions would you make to reduce the amount of automobile emissions?

SECTION REVIEW

1. How has the Earth's climate changed over time? What might have caused these changes?

2. Explain how the greenhouse effect warms the Earth.

3. What are two ways that humans contribute to the increase in carbon dioxide levels in the atmosphere?

4. **Analyzing Relationships** How will the warming of the Earth affect agriculture in different parts of the world?

internet**connect**

SCi*LINKS*
NSTA

TOPIC: Changes in Climate
GO TO: www.scilinks.org
*sci*LINKS NUMBER: HSTE415

Skill Builder Lab

Biome Business

You have just been hired as an assistant to a world-famous botanist. You have been provided with climatographs for three biomes. A *climatograph* is a graph that shows the temperature and precipitation patterns for an area for a year.

You can use the information provided in the graphs to determine the type of climate in each biome. You also have a general map of the biomes, but nothing is labeled. Using this information, you must figure out what the environment will be like in each biome.

In this activity, you will use climatographs and maps to determine where you will be traveling. You can find the exact locations by tracing the general maps and matching them to the map at the bottom of the page.

Procedure

1. Look at each climatograph. The shaded areas show the average precipitation for the biome. The red line shows the average temperature.

2. Use the climatographs to determine the climate patterns for each biome. Compare the maps with the biome map on page 74 to find the exact location of each region.

Analysis

3. Describe the precipitation patterns of each biome by answering the following questions:
   a. When does it rain the most in this biome?
   b. Do you think the biome is relatively dry, or do you think it rains a lot?

4. Describe the temperature patterns of each biome by answering the following questions:
   a. What are the warmest months of the year?
   b. Does the biome seem to have temperature cycles, like seasons, or is the temperature almost always the same?
   c. Do you think the biome is warm or cool? Explain your answer.

5. Name each biome.

6. Where is each biome located?

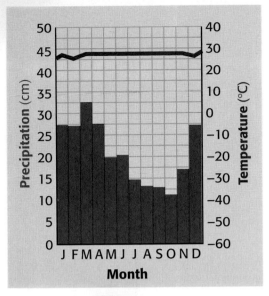

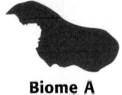

Biome A

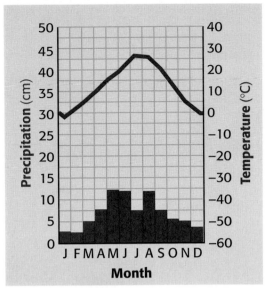

Biome C

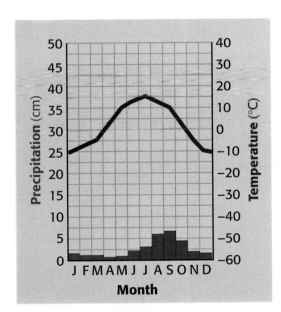

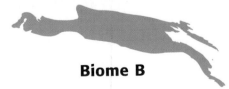

Biome B

Going Further

In a cardboard box no bigger than a shoe box, build a model of one of the biomes that you investigated. Include things to represent the biome, such as the plants and animals that inhabit the area. Use magazines, photographs, colored pencils, plastic figurines, clay, or whatever you like. Be creative!

Chapter Highlights

Vocabulary

weather *(p. 68)*

climate *(p. 68)*

latitude *(p. 69)*

prevailing winds *(p. 71)*

elevation *(p. 72)*

surface currents *(p. 73)*

Section Notes

- Weather is the condition of the atmosphere at a particular time and place. Climate is the average weather conditions in a certain area over a long period of time.

- Climate is determined by temperature and precipitation.

- Climate is controlled by factors such as latitude, elevation, wind patterns, local geography, and ocean surface currents.

- The amount of solar energy an area receives is determined by the area's latitude.

- The seasons are a result of the tilt of the Earth's axis and its path around the sun.

- The amount of moisture carried by prevailing winds affects the amount of precipitation that falls.

- As elevation increases, temperature decreases.

- Mountains affect the distribution of precipitation. The dry side of the mountain is called the rain shadow.

- As ocean surface currents move across the Earth, they redistribute warm and cool water. The temperature of the surface water affects the air temperature.

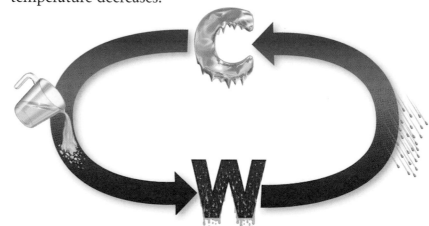

☑ Skills Check

Visual Understanding

THE SEASONS Seasons are determined by latitude. The diagram on page 70 shows how the tilt of the Earth affects how much solar energy an area receives as the Earth moves around the sun.

THE RAIN SHADOW The illustration on page 72 shows how the climates on two sides of a mountain can be very different. A mountain can affect the climate of areas nearby by influencing the amount of precipitation these areas receive.

LAND BIOMES OF THE EARTH Look back at Figure 10 on page 74 to review the distribution of the Earth's Land Biomes.

Vocabulary

biome *(p. 74)*

tropical zone *(p. 75)*

temperate zone *(p. 78)*

deciduous *(p. 78)*

evergreens *(p. 78)*

polar zone *(p. 80)*

microclimate *(p. 82)*

Section Notes

• The Earth is divided into three climate zones according to latitude—the tropical zone, the temperate zone, and the polar zone.

• The tropical zone is the zone around the equator. The tropical rain forest, tropical desert, and tropical savanna are in this zone.

• The temperate zone is the zone between the tropical zone and the polar zone. The temperate forest, temperate grassland, chaparral, and temperate desert are in this zone.

• The polar zones are the northernmost and southernmost zones. The taiga and tundra are in this zone.

Labs

For the Birds *(p. 109)*

Vocabulary

ice age *(p. 83)*

global warming *(p. 86)*

greenhouse effect *(p. 86)*

Section Notes

• Explanations for the occurrence of ice ages include changes in the Earth's orbit, volcanic eruptions, and plate tectonics and continental drift.

• Some scientists believe that global warming is occurring as a result of an increase in carbon dioxide from human activity.

• If global warming continues, it could drastically change climates, causing either floods or drought.

Labs

Global Impact *(p. 108)*

---

internet connect

GO TO: go.hrw.com

Visit the **HRW** Web site for a variety of learning tools related to this chapter. Just type in the keyword:

KEYWORD: HSTCLM

SCiLINKS
NSTA

GO TO: www.scilinks.org

Visit the **National Science Teachers Association** on-line Web site for Internet resources related to this chapter. Just type in the *sci*LINKS number for more information about the topic:

TOPIC:	*sci*LINKS NUMBER:
TOPIC: What Is Climate?	*sci*LINKS NUMBER: HSTE405
TOPIC: Climates of the World	*sci*LINKS NUMBER: HSTE410
TOPIC: Changes in Climate	*sci*LINKS NUMBER: HSTE415
TOPIC: Modeling Earth's Climate	*sci*LINKS NUMBER: HSTE420

Chapter Review

USING VOCABULARY

To complete the following sentences, choose the correct term from each pair of terms listed below.

1. ___?___ is the condition of the atmosphere in a certain area over a long period of time. *(Weather or Climate)*

2. ___?___ is the distance north and south from the equator measured in degrees. *(Longitude or Latitude)*

3. Savannas are grasslands located in the ___?___ zone between 23.5° north latitude and 23.5° south latitude. *(temperate or tropical)*

4. Trees that lose their leaves are found in a(n)___?___ forest. *(deciduous or evergreen)*

5. Frozen land in the polar zone is most often found in a ___?___. *(taiga or tundra)*

6. A rise in global temperatures due to an increase in carbon dioxide is called ___?___. *(global warming or the greenhouse effect)*

UNDERSTANDING CONCEPTS

Multiple Choice

7. The tilt of Earth as it orbits the sun causes
   a. global warming.
   b. different seasons.
   c. a rain shadow.
   d. the greenhouse effect.

8. What factor affects the prevailing winds as they blow across a continent, producing different climates?
   a. latitude   c. forests
   b. mountains   d. glaciers

9. What factor determines the amount of solar energy an area receives?
   a. latitude   c. mountains
   b. wind patterns   d. ocean currents

10. What climate zone has the coldest average temperature?
    a. tropical   c. temperate
    b. polar   d. tundra

11. What biome is not located in the tropical zone?
    a. rain forest   c. chaparral
    b. savanna   d. desert

12. What biome contains the greatest number of plant and animal species?
    a. rain forest   c. grassland
    b. temperate forest d. tundra

13. Which of the following is not a theory for the cause of ice ages?
    a. the Milankovitch theory
    b. volcanic eruptions
    c. plate tectonics
    d. the greenhouse effect

14. Which of the following is thought to contribute to global warming?
    a. wind patterns
    b. deforestation
    c. ocean surface currents
    d. microclimates

Short Answer

15. Why do higher latitudes receive less solar radiation than lower latitudes?

16. How does wind influence precipitation patterns?

17. Give an example of a microclimate. What causes the unique temperature and precipitation characteristics of this area?

18. How have desert plants and animals adapted to this biome?

19. How are tundra and deserts similar?

Concept Mapping

20. Use the following terms to create a concept map: climate, global warming, deforestation, greenhouse effect, flooding.

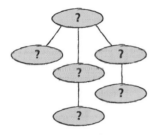

CRITICAL THINKING AND PROBLEM SOLVING

Write one or two sentences to answer the following questions:

21. Explain how ocean surface currents are responsible for milder climates.

22. In your own words, explain how a change in the Earth's orbit can affect the Earth's climates as proposed by Milutin Milankovitch.

23. Explain why the climate differs drastically on each side of the Rocky Mountains.

24. What are some steps you and your family can take to reduce the amount of carbon dioxide that is released into the atmosphere?

MATH IN SCIENCE

25. If the air temperature near the shore of a lake measures 24°C, and if the temperature increases by 0.05°C every 10 m traveled away from the lake, what would the air temperature be 1 km from the lake?

INTERPRETING GRAPHICS

The following illustration shows the Earth's orbit around the sun.

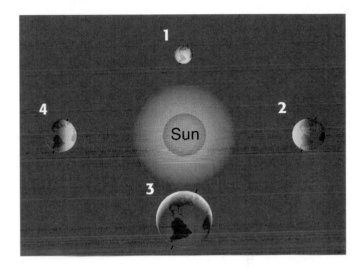

26. At what position, **1, 2, 3,** or **4,** is it spring in the Southern Hemisphere?

27. At what position does the South Pole receive almost 24 hours of daylight?

28. Explain what is happening in each climate zone in both the Northern Hemisphere and Southern Hemisphere at position **4.**

Reading Check-up

Take a minute to review your answers to the Pre-Reading Questions found at the bottom of page 66. Have your answers changed? If necessary, revise your answers based on what you have learned since you began this chapter.

Blame "The Child"

El Niño, which is Spanish for "the child," is the name of a weather event that occurs in the Pacific Ocean. Every 2 to 12 years, the interaction between the ocean surface and atmospheric winds creates El Niño. This event influences weather patterns in many regions of the world.

Difficult Breathing

For Indonesia and Malaysia, El Niño meant droughts and forest fires in 1998. Thousands of people in these countries suffered from respiratory ailments from breathing the smoke caused by these fires. Heavy rains in San Francisco created extremely high mold-spore counts. These spores cause problems for people with allergies. The spore count in February in San Francisco is usually between 0 and 100. In 1998, the count was often higher than 8,000!

Rodent Invasion

In areas where El Niño creates heavy rains, the result is lush vegetation. This lush vegetation provides even more food and shelter for rodents. As the rodent population increases, so does the threat of the diseases they spread. In states like Arizona, Colorado, and New Mexico, this means there is a greater chance among humans of contracting hantaviral pulmonary syndrome (HPS).

HPS is carried by deer mice and remains in their urine and feces. People are infected when they inhale dust contaminated with mouse feces or urine. Once infected, a person experiences flulike symptoms that can sometimes lead to fatal kidney or lung disease.

More Rodents and Insects

Heavy rains near Los Angeles might encourage a rodent-population explosion in the mountains east of the city. If so, there could be an increase in the number of rodents infected with bubonic plague. More infected rodents means more infected fleas, which carry bubonic plague to humans.

Ticks and mosquitoes could also increase in number. These insects can spread disease too. For example, ticks can carry Lyme disease, ehrlichiosis, babesiosis, and Rocky Mountain spotted fever. Mosquitoes can spread malaria, dengue fever, encephalitis, and Rift Valley fever.

◄ If this flea carries bubonic plague bacteria, just one bite can infect a person.

What About Camping?

Because all of these diseases can be fatal to humans, people must take precautions. Camping in the great outdoors increases the risk of infection. Campers should steer clear of rodents and their burrows. Don't forget to dust family pets with flea powder, and don't let them roam free. Try to remember that an ounce of prevention is worth a pound of cure.

Find Out More

► How do you think El Niño affects the fish and mammals that live in the ocean? Write your answer in your ScienceLog, and then do some research to see if you are correct.

Science, Technology, and Society

Some Say Fire, Some Say Ice . . .

The Earth's climate has undergone many drastic changes. For example, 6,000 years ago in the part of North Africa that is now a desert, hippos, crocodiles, and early Stone Age people shared shallow lakes that covered the area. Grasslands stretched as far as the eye could see.

Scientists have known for many years that Earth's climate has changed. What they didn't know was why. Using supercomputers and complex computer programs, scientists may now be able to explain why North Africa's lakes and grasslands became a desert. And that information may be useful for predicting future heat waves and ice ages.

Climate Models

Scientists who study Earth's atmosphere have developed climate models to try to imitate Earth's climate. A climate model is like a very complicated recipe with thousands of ingredients. These models do not make exact predictions about future climates, but they do estimate what might happen.

What ingredients are included in a climate model? One important ingredient is the level of greenhouse gases (especially carbon dioxide) in the atmosphere. Land and ocean water temperatures from around the globe are other ingredients. So is information about clouds, cloud cover, snow, and ice cover. And in more recent models, scientists have included information about ocean currents.

A Challenge to Scientists

Earth's atmosphere-ocean climate system is extremely complex. One challenge for scientists is to understand all the system's parts. Another is to understand how those parts work together. But understanding Earth's climate system is critical. An accurate climate model should help scientists predict heat waves, floods, and droughts.

Even the best available climate models must be improved. The more information scientists can include in a climate model, the more accurate the results. Today data are available from more locations, and scientists need more-powerful computers to process all the data.

As more-powerful computers are developed to handle all the data in a climate model, scientists' understanding of Earth's climate changes will improve. This knowledge should help scientists better predict the impact human activities have on global climate. And these models could help scientists prevent some of the worst effects of climate change, such as global warming or another ice age.

▲ *This meteorologist is using a high-powered supercomputer to do climate modeling.*

A Challenge for You

▶ Earth's oceans are a major part of the climate model. Find out some of the ways oceans affect climate. Do you think human activities are changing the oceans?

SAFETY FIRST!

Exploring, inventing, and investigating are essential to the study of science. However, these activities can also be dangerous. To make sure that your experiments and explorations are safe, you must be aware of a variety of safety guidelines.

You have probably heard of the saying, "It is better to be safe than sorry." This is particularly true in a science classroom where experiments and explorations are being performed. Being uninformed and careless can result in serious injuries. Don't take chances with your own safety or with anyone else's.

Following are important guidelines for staying safe in the science classroom. Your teacher may also have safety guidelines and tips that are specific to your classroom and laboratory. Take the time to be safe.

Safety Rules!

Start Out Right

Always get your teacher's permission before attempting any laboratory exploration. Read the procedures carefully, and pay particular attention to safety information and caution statements. If you are unsure about what a safety symbol means, look it up or ask your teacher. You cannot be too careful when it comes to safety. If an accident does occur, inform your teacher immediately, regardless of how minor you think the accident is.

If you are instructed to note the odor of a substance, wave the fumes toward your nose with your hand. Never put your nose close to the source.

Safety Symbols

All of the experiments and investigations in this book and their related worksheets include important safety symbols to alert you to particular safety concerns. Become familiar with these symbols so that when you see them, you will know what they mean and what to do. It is important that you read this entire safety section to learn about specific dangers in the laboratory.

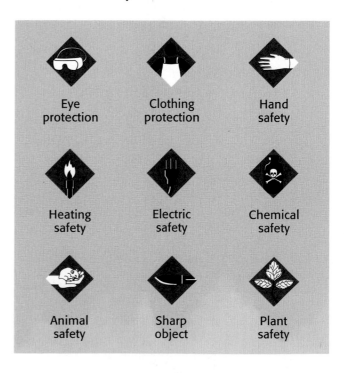

Eye protection

Clothing protection

Hand safety

Heating safety

Electric safety

Chemical safety

Animal safety

Sharp object

Plant safety

Eye Safety

Wear safety goggles when working around chemicals, acids, bases, or any type of flame or heating device. Wear safety goggles any time there is even the slightest chance that harm could come to your eyes. If any substance gets into your eyes, notify your teacher immediately, and flush your eyes with running water for at least 15 minutes. Treat any unknown chemical as if it were a dangerous chemical. Never look directly into the sun. Doing so could cause permanent blindness.

Avoid wearing contact lenses in a laboratory situation. Even if you are wearing safety goggles, chemicals can get between the contact lenses and your eyes. If your doctor requires that you wear contact lenses instead of glasses, wear eye-cup safety goggles in the lab.

Safety Equipment

Know the locations of the nearest fire alarms and any other safety equipment, such as fire blankets and eyewash fountains, as identified by your teacher, and know the procedures for using them.

Be extra careful when using any glassware. When adding a heavy object to a graduated cylinder, tilt the cylinder so the object slides slowly to the bottom.

Neatness

Keep your work area free of all unnecessary books and papers. Tie back long hair, and secure loose sleeves or other loose articles of clothing, such as ties and bows. Remove dangling jewelry. Don't wear open-toed shoes or sandals in the laboratory. Never eat, drink, or apply cosmetics in a laboratory setting. Food, drink, and cosmetics can easily become contaminated with dangerous materials.

Certain hair products (such as aerosol hair spray) are flammable and should not be worn while working near an open flame. Avoid wearing hair spray or hair gel on lab days.

Sharp/Pointed Objects

Use knives and other sharp instruments with extreme care. Never cut objects while holding them in your hands. Place objects on a suitable work surface for cutting.

Heat

Wear safety goggles when using a heating device or a flame. Whenever possible, use an electric hot plate as a heat source instead of an open flame. When heating materials in a test tube, always angle the test tube away from yourself and others. In order to avoid burns, wear heat-resistant gloves whenever instructed to do so.

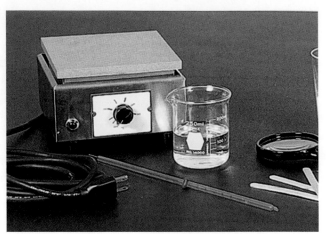

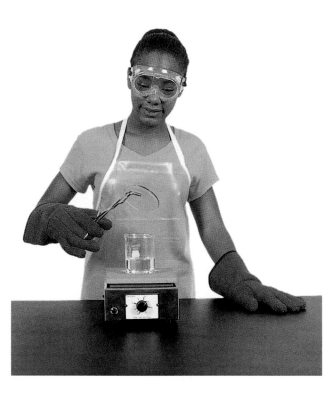

Chemicals

Wear safety goggles when handling any potentially dangerous chemicals, acids, or bases. If a chemical is unknown, handle it as you would a dangerous chemical. Wear an apron and safety gloves when working with acids or bases or whenever you are told to do so. If a spill gets on your skin or clothing, rinse it off immediately with water for at least 5 minutes while calling to your teacher.

Never mix chemicals unless your teacher tells you to do so. Never taste, touch, or smell chemicals unless you are specifically directed to do so. Before working with a flammable liquid or gas, check for the presence of any source of flame, spark, or heat.

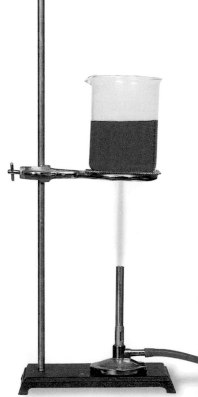

Electricity

Be careful with electrical cords. When using a microscope with a lamp, do not place the cord where it could trip someone. Do not let cords hang over a table edge in a way that could cause equipment to fall if the cord is accidentally pulled. Do not use equipment with damaged cords. Be sure your hands are dry and that the electrical equipment is in the "off" position before plugging it in. Turn off and unplug electrical equipment when you are finished.

Animal Safety

Always obtain your teacher's permission before bringing any animal into the school building. Handle animals only as your teacher directs. Always treat animals carefully and with respect. Wash your hands thoroughly after handling any animal.

Plant Safety

Do not eat any part of a plant or plant seed used in the laboratory. Wash hands thoroughly after handling any part of a plant. When in nature, do not pick any wild plants unless your teacher instructs you to do so.

Glassware

Examine all glassware before use. Be sure that glassware is clean and free of chips and cracks. Report damaged glassware to your teacher. Glass containers used for heating should be made of heat-resistant glass.

Boiling Over!

Safety Industries, Inc., would like to offer the public safer alternatives to the mercury thermometer. Many communities have complained that the glass thermometers are easy to break, and people are concerned about mercury poisoning. As a result, we would like your team of inventors to come up with a workable prototype that uses water instead of mercury. Safety Industries would like to offer a contract to the team that comes up with the best substitute for a mercury thermometer. In this activity, you will design and test your own water thermometer. Good luck!

Ask a Question

1. What conditions cause the liquid to rise in a thermometer? How can I use this information to build a thermometer?

Form a Hypothesis

2. Brainstorm with a classmate to design a thermometer that requires only water. Sketch your design in your ScienceLog. Write a one-sentence hypothesis that describes how your thermometer will work.

Test the Hypothesis

3. Follow your design to build a thermometer using only materials from the materials list. Like a mercury thermometer, your thermometer will need a bulb and a tube. However, the liquid in your thermometer will be water.

4. To test your design, place the aluminum pie pan on a hot plate. Carefully pour water into the pan until it is halfway full. Allow the water to heat.

5. Put on your gloves, and carefully place the "bulb" of your thermometer in the hot water. Observe the water level in the tube. Does it rise?

6. If the water level does not rise, adjust your design as necessary, and repeat steps 3–5. When the water level does rise, sketch your final design in your ScienceLog.

7. After you finalize your design, you must calibrate your thermometer with a laboratory thermometer by taping an index card to the thermometer tube so that the entire part of the tube protruding from the "bulb" of the thermometer touches the card.

Materials

- heat-resistant gloves
- aluminum pie pan
- hot plate
- water
- assorted containers, such as plastic bottles, soda cans, film canisters, medicine bottles, test tubes, balloons, and yogurt containers with lids
- assorted tubes, such as clear inflexible plastic straws or 5 mm diameter plastic tubing, 30 cm long
- modeling clay
- food coloring
- pitcher
- transparent tape
- index card
- Celsius thermometer
- a paper cone-shaped filter or funnel
- 2 large plastic-foam cups
- ice cubes
- metric ruler

8. Place the cone-shaped filter or funnel into the plastic-foam cup. Carefully pour hot water from the hot plate into the filter or funnel. Be sure that no water splashes or spills.

9. Place your own thermometer and a laboratory thermometer in the hot water. Mark the water level on the index card as it rises. Observe and record the temperature on the laboratory thermometer, and write this value on the card beside the mark.

10. Repeat steps 8–9 with warm water from the faucet.

11. Repeat steps 8–9 with ice water.

12. Divide the markings on the index card into equally sized increments, and write the corresponding temperatures on the index card.

Analyze the Results

13. How effective is your thermometer at measuring temperature?

14. Compare your thermometer design with other students' designs. How would you modify your design to make your thermometer measure temperature even better?

Draw Conclusions

15. Take a class vote to see which design should be chosen for a contract with Safety Industries. Why was this thermometer chosen? How did it differ from other designs in the class?

Go Fly a Bike!

Your friend Daniel just invented a bicycle that can fly! Trouble is, the bike can fly only when the wind speed is between 3 m/s and 10 m/s. If the wind is not blowing hard enough, the bike won't get enough lift to rise into the air, and if the wind is blowing too hard, the bike is difficult to control. Daniel needs to know if he can fly his bike today. Can you build a device that can estimate how fast the wind is blowing?

Ask a Question

1. How can I construct a device to measure wind speed?

Construct an Anemometer

2. Cut off the rolled edges of all five paper cups. This will make them lighter, so that they can spin more easily.

3. Measure and place four equally spaced markings 1 cm below the rim of one of the paper cups.

4. Use the hole punch to punch a hole at each mark so that the cup has four equally spaced holes. Use the sharp pencil to carefully punch a hole in the center of the bottom of the cup.

5. Push a straw through two opposite holes in the side of the cup.

6. Repeat step 5 for the other two holes. The straws should form an X.

7. Measure 3 cm from the bottom of the remaining paper cups, and mark each spot with a dot.

8. At each dot, punch a hole in the paper cups with the hole punch.

9. Color the outside of one of the four cups.

10. Slide a cup on one of the straws by pushing the straw through the punched hole. Rotate the cup so that the bottom faces to the right.

Materials

- scissors
- 5 small paper cups
- metric ruler
- hole punch
- 2 straight plastic straws
- colored marker
- small stapler
- thumbtack
- sharp pencil with an eraser
- modeling clay
- masking tape
- watch or clock that indicates seconds

11. Fold the end of the straw, and staple it to the inside of the cup directly across from the hole.

12. Repeat steps 10–11 for each of the remaining cups.

13. Push the tack through the intersection of the two straws.

14. Push the eraser end of a pencil through the bottom hole in the center cup. Push the tack as far as it will go into the end of the eraser.

15. Push the sharpened end of the pencil into some modeling clay to form a base. This will allow the device to stand up without being knocked over, as shown at right.

16. Blow into the cups so that they spin. Adjust the tack so that the cups can freely spin without wobbling or falling apart. Congratulations! You have just constructed an anemometer.

Conduct an Experiment

17. Find a suitable area outside to place the anemometer vertically on a surface away from objects that would obstruct the wind, such as buildings and trees.

18. Mark the surface at the base of the anemometer with masking tape. Label the tape "starting point."

19. Hold the colored cup over the starting point while your partner holds the watch.

20. Release the colored cup. At the same time, your partner should look at the watch or clock. As the cups spin, count the number of times the colored cup crosses the starting point in 10 seconds.

Analyze the Results

21. How many times did the colored cup cross the starting point in 10 seconds?

22. Divide your answer in step 21 by 10 to get the number of revolutions in 1 second.

23. Measure the diameter of your anemometer (the distance between the outside edges of two opposite cups) in centimeters. Multiply this number by 3.14 to get the circumference of the circle made by the cups of your anemometer.

24. Multiply your answer from step 23 by the number of revolutions per second (step 22). Divide that answer by 100 to get wind speed in meters per second.

25. Compare your results with those of your classmates. Did you get the same result? What could account for any slight differences in your results?

Draw Conclusions

26. Could Daniel fly his bicycle today? Why or why not?

Watching the Weather

Imagine that you own a private consulting firm that helps people plan for big occasions, such as weddings, parties, and celebrity events. One of your duties is making sure the weather doesn't put a damper on your clients' plans. In order to provide the best service possible, you have taken a crash course in reading weather maps. Will the celebrity golf match have to be delayed on account of rain? Will the wedding ceremony have to be moved inside so the blushing bride doesn't get soaked? It is your job to say "yea" or "nay."

Procedure

1. Study the station model and legend shown on the next page. You will use the legend to interpret the weather map on the final page of this activity.

2. Weather data is represented on a weather map by a station model. A station model is a small circle that shows the location of the weather station along with a set of symbols and numbers around the circle that represent the data collected at the weather station. Study the table below.

Weather-Map Symbols					
Weather conditions		**Cloud cover**		**Wind speed (mph)**	
• •	Light rain	○	No clouds	◎	Calm
∴	Moderate rain	◑	One-tenth or less		3–8
∴∴	Heavy rain	◕	Two- to three-tenths		9–14
,	Drizzle	◗	Broken		15–20
* *	Light snow	◍	Nine-tenths		21–25
**	Moderate snow	●	Overcast		32–37
℞	Thunderstorm	⊗	Sky obscured		44–48
⌒∿	Freezing rain		**Special Symbols**		55–60
∞	Haze	▲▲▲▲	Cold front		66–71
═	Fog	●●●●	Warm front		
		H	High pressure		
		L	Low pressure		
		∫	Hurricane		

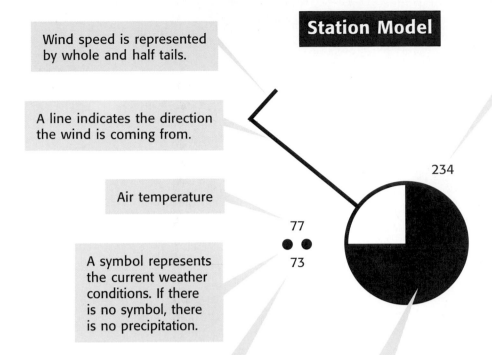

Station Model

Wind speed is represented by whole and half tails.

A line indicates the direction the wind is coming from.

Air temperature

A symbol represents the current weather conditions. If there is no symbol, there is no precipitation.

234

77

73

Dew point temperature

Shading indicates the cloud coverage.

Atmospheric pressure in millibars (mbar). This number has been shortened on the station model. To read the number properly you must follow a few simple rules.

- If the first number is greater than 5, place a 9 in front of the number and a decimal point between the last two digits.
- If the first number is less than or equal to 5, place a 10 in front of the number and a decimal point between the last two digits.

Interpreting Station Models

The station model below is for Boston, Massachusetts. The current temperature in Boston is 42°F, and the dew point is 39°F. The barometric pressure is 1011.0 mbar. The sky is overcast, and there is a moderate rainfall. The wind is coming from the southwest at 15–20 mph.

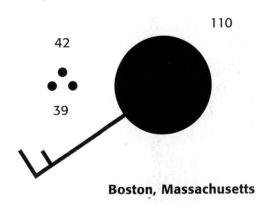

110

42

39

Boston, Massachusetts

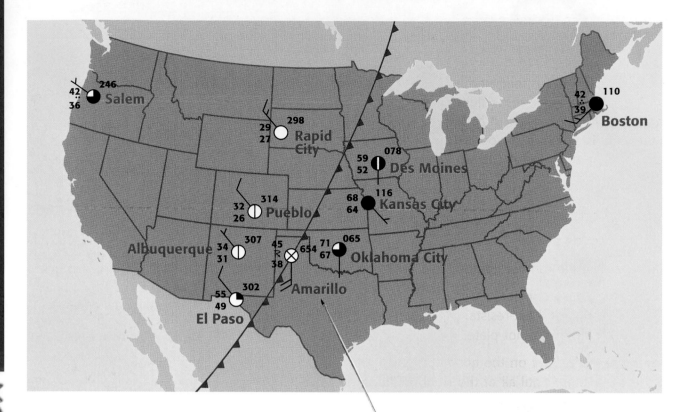

Analysis

3. Based on the weather for the entire United States, what time of year is it? Explain your answer.

4. Interpret the station model for Salem, Oregon. What is the temperature, dew point, cloud coverage, wind direction, wind speed, and atmospheric pressure? Is there any precipitation? If so, what kind?

5. What is happening to wind direction, temperature, and pressure as the cold front approaches? as it passes?

6. Interpret the station model for Amarillo, Texas.

Let It Snow!

While an inch of rain might be good for your garden, 7 or 8 cm could cause an unwelcome flood. But what about snow? How much snow is too much? A blizzard might drop 40 cm of snow overnight. Sure it's up to your knees, but how does this much snow compare with rain? This activity will help you find out.

Materials

- 150 mL of shaved ice
- 100 mL beaker
- metric ruler
- heat-resistant gloves
- hot plate
- graduated cylinder

Procedure

1. Pour 50 mL of shaved ice into your beaker. Do not pack the ice into the beaker. This ice will represent your snowfall.

2. Use the ruler to measure the height of the snow in the beaker.

3. Turn on the hot plate to a low setting.
   Caution: Wear heat-resistant gloves and goggles when working with the hot plate.

4. Place the beaker on the hot plate, and leave it there until all of the snow melts.

5. Pour the water into the graduated cylinder, and record the height and volume of the water in your ScienceLog.

6. Repeat steps 1–5 two more times.

Analysis

7. What was the difference in height before and after the snow melted in each of your three trials? What was the average difference?

8. Why did the volume change after the ice melted?

9. In this activity, what was the ratio of snow height to water height?

10. Use the ratio you found in step 9 to calculate how much water 50 cm of this snow would produce. Use the following equation to help.

$$\frac{\text{measured height of snow}}{\text{measured height of water}} = \frac{\text{50 cm of snow}}{\text{? cm of water}}$$

11. Why is it important to know the water content of a snowfall?

Going Further

Shaved ice isn't really snow. Research to find out how much water real snow would produce. Does every snowfall produce the same ratio of snow height to water depth?

Global Impact

For years scientists have debated the topic of global warming. Is the temperature of the Earth actually getting warmer? Sample sizes are a very important factor in any scientific study. In this activity, you will examine a chart to determine if the data indicate any trends. Be sure to notice how much the trends seem to change as you analyze different sets of data.

Materials

- 4 colored pencils
- metric ruler

Procedure

1. Look at the chart below. It shows average global temperatures recorded over the last 100 years.

2. Draw a graph in your ScienceLog. Label the horizontal axis "Time," and mark the grid in 5-year intervals. Label the vertical axis "Temperature (°C)," with values ranging from 13°C to 15°C.

3. Starting with 1900, use the numbers in red to plot the temperature in 20-year intervals. Connect the dots with straight lines.

4. Using a ruler, estimate the overall slope of temperatures, and draw a red line to represent the slope.

5. Using different colors, plot the temperatures at 10-year intervals and 5-year intervals on the same graph. Connect each set of dots, and draw the average slope for each set.

Analysis

6. Examine your completed graph, and explain any trends you see in the graphed data. Was there an increase or a decrease in average temperature over the last 100 years?

7. What differences did you see in each set of graphed data? what similarities?

8. What conclusions can you draw from the data you graphed in this activity?

9. What would happen if your graph were plotted in 1-year intervals? Try it!

Average Global Temperatures											
Year	°C	Year	°C	Year	°C	Year	°C	Year	°C	Year	°C
1900	14.0	1917	13.6	1934	14.0	1951	14.0	1968	13.9	1985	14.1
1901	13.9	1918	13.6	1935	13.9	1952	14.0	1969	14.0	1986	14.2
1902	13.8	1919	13.8	1936	14.0	1953	14.1	1970	14.0	1987	14.3
1903	13.6	1920	13.8	1937	14.1	1954	13.9	1971	13.9	1988	14.4
1904	13.5	1921	13.9	1938	14.1	1955	13.9	1972	13.9	1989	14.2
1905	13.7	1922	13.9	1939	14.0	1956	13.8	1973	14.2	1990	14.5
1906	13.8	1923	13.8	1940	14.1	1957	14.1	1974	13.9	1991	14.4
1907	13.6	1924	13.8	1941	14.1	1958	14.1	1975	14.0	1992	14.1
1908	13.7	1925	13.8	1942	14.1	1959	14.0	1976	13.8	1993	14.2
1909	13.7	1926	14.1	1943	14.0	1960	14.0	1977	14.2	1994	14.3
1910	13.7	1927	14.0	1944	14.1	1961	14.1	1978	14.1	1995	14.5
1911	13.7	1928	14.0	1945	14.0	1962	14.0	1979	14.1	1996	14.4
1912	13.7	1929	13.8	1946	14.0	1963	14.0	1980	14.3	1997	14.4
1913	13.8	1930	13.9	1947	14.1	1964	13.7	1981	14.4	1998	14.5
1914	14.0	1931	14.0	1948	14.0	1965	13.8	1982	14.1	1999	
1915	14.0	1932	14.0	1949	13.9	1966	13.9	1983	14.3	2000	
1916	13.8	1933	13.9	1950	13.8	1967	14.0	1984	14.1	2001	

For the Birds

You and a partner have a new business building birdhouses. But your first clients have told you that birds do not want to live in the birdhouses you have made. The clients want their money back unless you can solve the problem. You need to come up with a solution right away!

You remember reading an article about microclimates in a science magazine. Cities often heat up because the pavement and buildings absorb so much solar radiation. Maybe the houses are too warm! How can the houses be kept cooler?

You decide to investigate the roofs; after all, changing the roofs would be a lot easier than building new houses. In order to help your clients and the birds, you decide to test different roof colors and materials to see how these variables affect a roof's ability to absorb the sun's rays.

One partner will test the color, and the other partner will test the materials. You will then share your results and make a recommendation together.

Materials

- 4 pieces of cardboard
- black, white, and light-blue tempera paint
- 4 Celsius thermometers
- watch or clock
- beige or tan wood
- beige or tan rubber

Part A: Color Test

Ask a Question

1. What color would be the best choice for the roof of a birdhouse?

Form a Hypothesis

2. In your ScienceLog, write down the color you think will keep a birdhouse coolest.

Test the Hypothesis

3. Paint one piece of cardboard black, another piece white, and a third light blue.

4. After the paint has dried, take the three pieces of cardboard outside, and place a thermometer on each piece.

5. In an area where there is no shade, place each piece at the same height so that all three receive the same amount of sun-light. Leave the pieces in the sunlight for 15 minutes.

6. Leave a fourth thermometer outside in the shade to measure the temperature of the air.

7. In your ScienceLog, record the reading of the thermometer on each piece of cardboard. Also record the outside temperature.

Analyze the Results

8. Did each of the three thermometers record the same temperature after 15 minutes? Explain.

9. Were the temperature readings on each of the three pieces of cardboard the same as the reading for the outside temperature? Explain.

Draw Conclusions

10. How do your observations compare with your hypothesis?

Part B: Material Test

Ask a Question

11. Which material would be the best choice for the roof of a birdhouse?

Form a Hypothesis

12. In your ScienceLog, write down the material you think will keep a birdhouse coolest.

Test the Hypothesis

13. Take the rubber, wood, and the fourth piece of cardboard outside, and place a thermometer on each.

14. In an area where there is no shade, place each material at the same height so that they all receive the same amount of sunlight. Leave the materials in the sunlight for 15 minutes.

15. Leave a fourth thermometer outside in the shade to measure the temperature of the air.

16. In your ScienceLog, record the temperature of each material. Also record the outside temperature.

Analyze the Results

17. Did each of the thermometers on the three materials record the same temperature after 15 minutes? Explain.

18. Were the temperature readings on the rubber, wood, and cardboard the same as the reading for the outside temperature? Explain.

Draw Conclusions

19. How do your observations compare with your hypothesis?

Sharing Information (Parts A and B)

Communicate Results

After you and your partner have finished your investigations, take a few minutes to share your results. Then work together to design a new roof.

20. Which material would you use to build the roofs for your birdhouses? Why?

21. Which color would you use to paint the new roofs? Why?

Going Further

Make three different-colored samples for each of the three materials. When you measure the temperatures for each sample, how do the colors compare for each material? Is the same color best for all three materials? How do your results compare with what you concluded in steps 20 and 21 of this activity? What's more important, color or material?

Concept Mapping: A Way to Bring Ideas Together

What Is a Concept Map?

Have you ever tried to tell someone about a book or a chapter you've just read and found that you can remember only a few isolated words and ideas? Or maybe you've memorized facts for a test and then weeks later discovered you're not even sure what topics those facts covered.

In both cases, you may have understood the ideas or concepts by themselves but not in relation to one another. If you could somehow link the ideas together, you would probably understand them better and remember them longer. This is something a concept map can help you do. A concept map is a way to see how ideas or concepts fit together. It can help you see the "big picture."

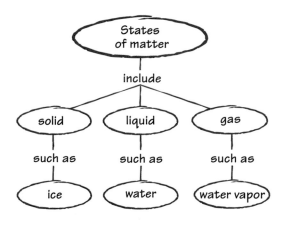

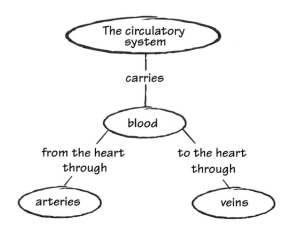

How to Make a Concept Map

1 Make a list of the main ideas or concepts.

It might help to write each concept on its own slip of paper. This will make it easier to rearrange the concepts as many times as necessary to make sense of how the concepts are connected. After you've made a few concept maps this way, you can go directly from writing your list to actually making the map.

2 Arrange the concepts in order from the most general to the most specific.

Put the most general concept at the top and circle it. Ask yourself, "How does this concept relate to the remaining concepts?" As you see the relationships, arrange the concepts in order from general to specific.

3 Connect the related concepts with lines.

4 On each line, write an action word or short phrase that shows how the concepts are related.

Look at the concept maps on this page, and then see if you can make one for the following terms:

plants, water, photosynthesis, carbon dioxide, sun's energy

One possible answer is provided at right, but don't look at it until you try the concept map yourself.

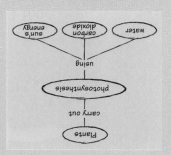

SI Measurement

The International System of Units, or SI, is the standard system of measurement used by many scientists. Using the same standards of measurement makes it easier for scientists to communicate with one another.

SI works by combining prefixes and base units. Each base unit can be used with different prefixes to define smaller and larger quantities. The table below lists common SI prefixes.

SI Prefixes

Prefix	Abbreviation	Factor	Example
kilo-	k	1,000	kilogram, 1 kg = 1,000 g
hecto-	h	100	hectoliter, 1 hL = 100 L
deka-	da	10	dekameter, 1 dam = 10 m
		1	meter, liter
deci-	d	0.1	decigram, 1 dg = 0.1 g
centi-	c	0.01	centimeter, 1 cm = 0.01 m
milli-	m	0.001	milliliter, 1 mL = 0.001 L
micro-	μ	0.000 001	micrometer, 1 μm = 0.000 001 m

SI Conversion Table

SI units	From SI to English	From English to SI
Length		
kilometer (km) = 1,000 m	1 km = 0.621 mi	1 mi = 1.609 km
meter (m) = 100 cm	1 m = 3.281 ft	1 ft = 0.305 m
centimeter (cm) = 0.01 m	1 cm = 0.394 in.	1 in. = 2.540 cm
millimeter (mm) = 0.001 m	1 mm = 0.039 in.	
micrometer (μm) = 0.000 001 m		
nanometer (nm) = 0.000 000 001 m		
Area		
square kilometer (km^2) = 100 hectares	1 km^2 = 0.386 mi^2	1 mi^2 = 2.590 km^2
hectare (ha) = 10,000 m^2	1 ha = 2.471 acres	1 acre = 0.405 ha
square meter (m^2) = 10,000 cm^2	1 m^2 = 10.765 ft^2	1 ft^2 = 0.093 m^2
square centimeter (cm^2) = 100 mm^2	1 cm^2 = 0.155 in.^{2}	1 in.^{2} = 6.452 cm^2
Volume		
liter (L) = 1,000 mL = 1 dm^3	1 L = 1.057 fl qt	1 fl qt = 0.946 L
milliliter (mL) = 0.001 L = 1 cm^3	1 mL = 0.034 fl oz	1 fl oz = 29.575 mL
microliter (μL) = 0.000 001 L		
Mass		
kilogram (kg) = 1,000 g	1 kg = 2.205 lb	1 lb = 0.454 kg
gram (g) = 1,000 mg	1 g = 0.035 oz	1 oz = 28.349 g
milligram (mg) = 0.001 g		
microgram (μg) = 0.000 001 g		

Temperature Scales

Temperature can be expressed using three different scales: Fahrenheit, Celsius, and Kelvin. The SI unit for temperature is the kelvin (K).

Although 0 K is much colder than 0°C, a change of 1 K is equal to a change of 1°C.

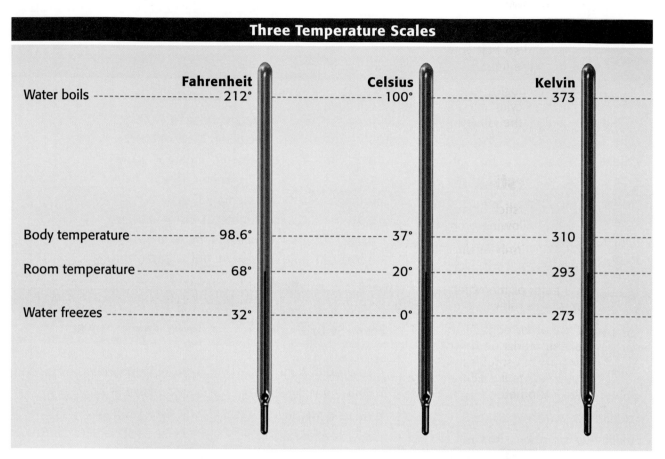

Three Temperature Scales

	Fahrenheit	Celsius	Kelvin
Water boils	212°	100°	373
Body temperature	98.6°	37°	310
Room temperature	68°	20°	293
Water freezes	32°	0°	273

Temperature Conversions Table

To convert	Use this equation:	Example
Celsius to Fahrenheit °C → °F	$°F = \left(\dfrac{9}{5} \times °C\right) + 32$	Convert 45°C to °F. $°F = \left(\dfrac{9}{5} \times 45°C\right) + 32 = 113°F$
Fahrenheit to Celsius °F → °C	$°C = \dfrac{5}{9} \times (°F - 32)$	Convert 68°F to °C. $°C = \dfrac{5}{9} \times (68°F - 32) = 20°C$
Celsius to Kelvin °C → K	$K = °C + 273$	Convert 45°C to K. $K = 45°C + 273 = 318 \text{ K}$
Kelvin to Celsius K → °C	$°C = K - 273$	Convert 32 K to °C. $°C = 32 \text{ K} - 273 = -241°C$

Measuring Skills

Using a Graduated Cylinder

When using a graduated cylinder to measure volume, keep the following procedures in mind:

1 Make sure the cylinder is on a flat, level surface.

2 Move your head so that your eye is level with the surface of the liquid.

3 Read the mark closest to the liquid level. On glass graduated cylinders, read the mark closest to the center of the curve in the liquid's surface.

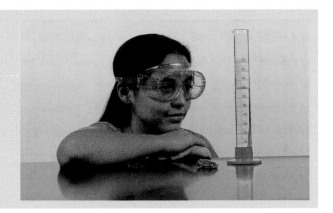

Using a Meterstick or Metric Ruler

When using a meterstick or metric ruler to measure length, keep the following procedures in mind:

1 Place the ruler firmly against the object you are measuring.

2 Align one edge of the object exactly with the zero end of the ruler.

3 Look at the other edge of the object to see which of the marks on the ruler is closest to that edge. **Note:** Each small slash between the centimeters represents a millimeter, which is one-tenth of a centimeter.

Using a Triple-Beam Balance

When using a triple-beam balance to measure mass, keep the following procedures in mind:

1 Make sure the balance is on a level surface.

2 Place all of the countermasses at zero. Adjust the balancing knob until the pointer rests at zero.

3 Place the object you wish to measure on the pan. **Caution:** Do not place hot objects or chemicals directly on the balance pan.

4 Move the largest countermass along the beam to the right until it is at the last notch that does not tip the balance. Follow the same procedure with the next-largest countermass. Then move the smallest countermass until the pointer rests at zero.

5 Add the readings from the three beams together to determine the mass of the object.

6 When determining the mass of crystals or powders, use a piece of filter paper. First find the mass of the paper. Then add the crystals or powder to the paper and re-measure. The actual mass of the crystals or powder is the total mass minus the mass of the paper. When finding the mass of liquids, first find the mass of the empty container. Then find the mass of the liquid and container together. The mass of the liquid is the total mass minus the mass of the container.

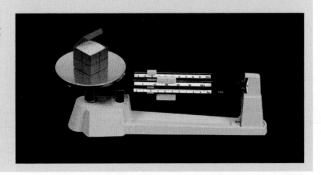

Scientific Method

The series of steps that scientists use to answer questions and solve problems is often called the **scientific method.** The scientific method is not a rigid procedure. Scientists may use all of the steps or just some of the steps of the scientific method. They may even repeat some of the steps. The goal of the scientific method is to come up with reliable answers and solutions.

Six Steps of the Scientific Method

1 **Ask a Question** Good questions come from careful **observations.** You make observations by using your senses to gather information. Sometimes you may use instruments, such as microscopes and telescopes, to extend the range of your senses. As you observe the natural world, you will discover that you have many more questions than answers. These questions drive the scientific method.

Questions beginning with *what, why, how,* and *when* are very important in focusing an investigation, and they often lead to a hypothesis. (You will learn what a hypothesis is in the next step.) Here is an example of a question that could lead to further investigation.

Question: How does acid rain affect plant growth?

2 **Form a Hypothesis** After you come up with a question, you need to turn the question into a **hypothesis.** A hypothesis is a clear statement of what you expect the answer to your question to be. Your hypothesis will represent your best "educated guess" based on your observations and what you already know. A good hypothesis is testable. If observations and information cannot be gathered or if an experiment cannot be designed to test your hypothesis, it is untestable, and the investigation can go no further.

Here is a hypothesis that could be formed from the question, "How does acid rain affect plant growth?"

Hypothesis: Acid rain causes plants to grow more slowly.

Notice that the hypothesis provides some specifics that lead to methods of testing. The hypothesis can also lead to predictions. A **prediction** is what you think will be the outcome of your experiment or data collection. Predictions are usually stated in an "if . . . then" format. For example, **if** meat is kept at room temperature, **then** it will spoil faster than meat kept in the refrigerator. More than one prediction can be made for a single hypothesis. Here is a sample prediction for the hypothesis that acid rain causes plants to grow more slowly.

Prediction: If a plant is watered with only acid rain (which has a pH of 4), then the plant will grow at half its normal rate.

3 **Test the Hypothesis** After you have formed a hypothesis and made a prediction, you should test your hypothesis. There are different ways to do this. Perhaps the most familiar way is to conduct a **controlled experiment.** A controlled experiment tests only one factor at a time. A controlled experiment has a **control group** and one or more **experimental groups.** All the factors for the control and experimental groups are the same except for one factor, which is called the **variable.** By changing only one factor, you can see the results of just that one change.

Sometimes, the nature of an investigation makes a controlled experiment impossible. For example, dinosaurs have been extinct for millions of years, and the Earth's core is surrounded by thousands of meters of rock. It would be difficult, if not impossible, to conduct controlled experiments on such things. Under such circumstances, a hypothesis may be tested by making detailed observations. Taking measurements is one way of making observations.

4 **Analyze the Results** After you have completed your experiments, made your observations, and collected your data, you must analyze all the information you have gathered. Tables and graphs are often used in this step to organize the data.

5 **Draw Conclusions** Based on the analysis of your data, you should conclude whether or not your results support your hypothesis. If your hypothesis is supported, you (or others) might want to repeat the observations or experiments to verify your results. If your hypothesis is not supported by the data, you may have to check your procedure for errors. You may even have to reject your hypothesis and make a new one. If you cannot draw a conclusion from your results, you may have to try the investigation again or carry out further observations or experiments.

Draw Conclusions

Do they support your hypothesis?

No

Yes

6 **Communicate Results** After any scientific investigation, you should report your results. By doing a written or oral report, you let others know what you have learned. They may want to repeat your investigation to see if they get the same results. Your report may even lead to another question, which in turn may lead to another investigation.

Test the Hypothesis

Analyze the Results

Communicate Results

APPENDIX

Scientific Method in Action

The scientific method is not a "straight line" of steps. It contains loops in which several steps may be repeated over and over again, while others may not be necessary. For example, sometimes scientists will find that testing one hypothesis raises new questions and new hypotheses to be tested. And sometimes, testing the hypothesis leads directly to a conclusion. Furthermore, the steps in the scientific method are not always used in the same order. Follow the steps in the diagram below, and see how many different directions the scientific method can take you.

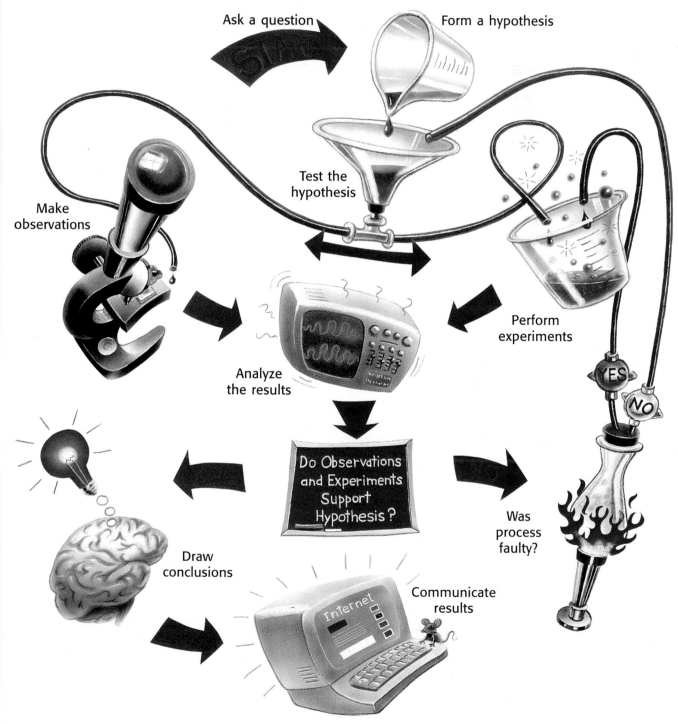

Making Charts and Graphs

Circle Graphs

A circle graph, or pie chart, shows how each group of data relates to all of the data. Each part of the circle represents a category of the data. The entire circle represents all of the data. For example, a biologist studying a hardwood forest in Wisconsin found that there were five different types of trees. The data table at right summarizes the biologist's findings.

Wisconsin Hardwood Trees	
Type of tree	Number found
Oak	600
Maple	750
Beech	300
Birch	1,200
Hickory	150
Total	3,000

How to Make a Circle Graph

1 In order to make a circle graph of this data, first find the percentage of each type of tree. To do this, divide the number of individual trees by the total number of trees and multiply by 100.

$$\frac{600 \text{ oak}}{3{,}000 \text{ trees}} \times 100 = 20\%$$

$$\frac{750 \text{ maple}}{3{,}000 \text{ trees}} \times 100 = 25\%$$

$$\frac{300 \text{ beech}}{3{,}000 \text{ trees}} \times 100 = 10\%$$

$$\frac{1{,}200 \text{ birch}}{3{,}000 \text{ trees}} \times 100 = 40\%$$

$$\frac{150 \text{ hickory}}{3{,}000 \text{ trees}} \times 100 = 5\%$$

2 Now determine the size of the pie shapes that make up the chart. Do this by multiplying each percentage by 360°. Remember that a circle contains 360°.

$20\% \times 360° = 72°$ $25\% \times 360° = 90°$
$10\% \times 360° = 36°$ $40\% \times 360° = 144°$
$5\% \times 360° = 18°$

3 Then check that the sum of the percentages is 100 and the sum of the degrees is 360.

$20\% + 25\% + 10\% + 40\% + 5\% = 100\%$
$72° + 90° + 36° + 144° + 18° = 360°$

4 Use a compass to draw a circle and mark its center.

5 Then use a protractor to draw angles of 72°, 90°, 36°, 144°, and 18° in the circle.

6 Finally, label each part of the graph, and choose an appropriate title.

A Community of Wisconsin Hardwood Trees

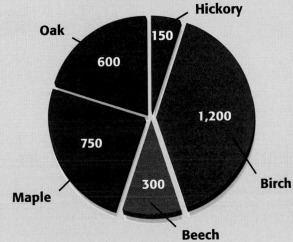

Line Graphs

Population of Appleton, 1900–2000	
Year	Population
1900	1,800
1920	2,500
1940	3,200
1960	3,900
1980	4,600
2000	5,300

Line graphs are most often used to demonstrate continuous change. For example, Mr. Smith's science class analyzed the population records for their hometown, Appleton, between 1900 and 2000. Examine the data at left.

Because the year and the population change, they are the *variables*. The population is determined by, or dependent on, the year. Therefore, the population is called the **dependent variable**, and the year is called the **independent variable**. Each set of data is called a **data pair**. To prepare a line graph, data pairs must first be organized in a table like the one at left.

How to Make a Line Graph

❶ Place the independent variable along the horizontal (*x*) axis. Place the dependent variable along the vertical (*y*) axis.

❷ Label the *x*-axis "Year" and the *y*-axis "Population." Look at your largest and smallest values for the population. Determine a scale for the *y*-axis that will provide enough space to show these values. You must use the same scale for the entire length of the axis. Find an appropriate scale for the *x*-axis too.

❸ Choose reasonable starting points for each axis.

❹ Plot the data pairs as accurately as possible.

❺ Choose a title that accurately represents the data.

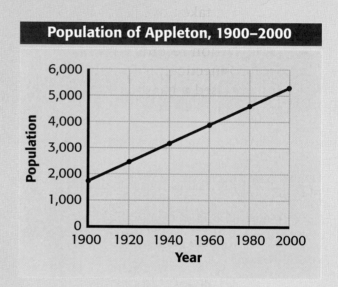

How to Determine Slope

Slope is the ratio of the change in the *y*-axis to the change in the *x*-axis, or "rise over run."

❶ Choose two points on the line graph. For example, the population of Appleton in 2000 was 5,300 people. Therefore, you can define point *a* as (2000, 5,300). In 1900, the population was 1,800 people. Define point *b* as (1900, 1,800).

❷ Find the change in the *y*-axis.
(*y* at point *a*) − (*y* at point *b*)
5,300 people − 1,800 people = 3,500 people

❸ Find the change in the *x*-axis.
(*x* at point *a*) − (*x* at point *b*)
2000 − 1900 = 100 years

❹ Calculate the slope of the graph by dividing the change in *y* by the change in *x*.

$$\text{slope} = \frac{\text{change in } y}{\text{change in } x}$$

$$\text{slope} = \frac{3{,}500 \text{ people}}{100 \text{ years}}$$

slope = 35 people per year

In this example, the population in Appleton increased by a fixed amount each year. The graph of this data is a straight line. Therefore, the relationship is **linear**. When the graph of a set of data is not a straight line, the relationship is **nonlinear**.

Using Algebra to Determine Slope

The equation in step 4 may also be arranged to be:

$$y = kx$$

where y represents the change in the y-axis, k represents the slope, and x represents the change in the x-axis.

$$slope = \frac{change\ in\ y}{change\ in\ x}$$

$$k = \frac{y}{x}$$

$$k \times x = \frac{y \times x}{x}$$

$$kx = y$$

Bar Graphs

Bar graphs are used to demonstrate change that is not continuous. These graphs can be used to indicate trends when the data are taken over a long period of time. A meteorologist gathered the precipitation records at right for Hartford, Connecticut, for April 1–15, 1996, and used a bar graph to represent the data.

Precipitation in Hartford, Connecticut April 1–15, 1996			
Date	Precipitation (cm)	Date	Precipitation (cm)
April 1	0.5	April 9	0.25
April 2	1.25	April 10	0.0
April 3	0.0	April 11	1.0
April 4	0.0	April 12	0.0
April 5	0.0	April 13	0.25
April 6	0.0	April 14	0.0
April 7	0.0	April 15	6.50
April 8	1.75		

How to Make a Bar Graph

❶ Use an appropriate scale and a reasonable starting point for each axis.

❷ Label the axes, and plot the data.

❸ Choose a title that accurately represents the data.

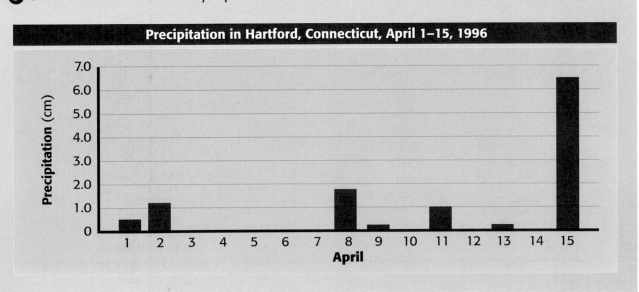

Math Refresher

Science requires an understanding of many math concepts. The following pages will help you review some important math skills.

Averages

An **average**, or **mean**, simplifies a list of numbers into a single number that *approximates* their value.

> **Example:** Find the average of the following set of numbers: 5, 4, 7, and 8.

Step 1: Find the sum.

$$5 + 4 + 7 + 8 = 24$$

Step 2: Divide the sum by the amount of numbers in your set. Because there are four numbers in this example, divide the sum by 4.

$$\frac{24}{4} = 6$$

The average, or mean, is **6.**

Ratios

A **ratio** is a comparison between numbers, and it is usually written as a fraction.

> **Example:** Find the ratio of thermometers to students if you have 36 thermometers and 48 students in your class.

Step 1: Make the ratio.

$$\frac{36 \text{ thermometers}}{48 \text{ students}}$$

Step 2: Reduce the fraction to its simplest form.

$$\frac{36}{48} = \frac{36 \div 12}{48 \div 12} = \frac{3}{4}$$

The ratio of thermometers to students is **3 to 4,** or $\frac{3}{4}$. The ratio may also be written in the form 3:4.

Proportions

A **proportion** is an equation that states that two ratios are equal.

$$\frac{3}{1} = \frac{12}{4}$$

To solve a proportion, first multiply across the equal sign. This is called cross-multiplication. If you know three of the quantities in a proportion, you can use cross-multiplication to find the fourth.

> **Example:** Imagine that you are making a scale model of the solar system for your science project. The diameter of Jupiter is 11.2 times the diameter of the Earth. If you are using a plastic-foam ball with a diameter of 2 cm to represent the Earth, what diameter does the ball representing Jupiter need to be?
>
> $$\frac{11.2}{1} = \frac{x}{2 \text{ cm}}$$

Step 1: Cross-multiply.

$$\frac{11.2}{1} \diagdown \!\!\!\!\diagup \frac{x}{2}$$

$$11.2 \times 2 = x \times 1$$

Step 2: Multiply.

$$22.4 = x \times 1$$

Step 3: Isolate the variable by dividing both sides by 1.

$$x = \frac{22.4}{1}$$

$$x = 22.4 \text{ cm}$$

You will need to use a ball with a diameter of **22.4 cm** to represent Jupiter.

Percentages

A **percentage** is a ratio of a given number to 100.

> **Example:** What is 85 percent of 40?

Step 1: Rewrite the percentage by moving the decimal point two places to the left.

$$.85$$

Step 2: Multiply the decimal by the number you are calculating the percentage of.

$$0.85 \times 40 = 34$$

85 percent of 40 is **34.**

Decimals

To **add** or **subtract decimals,** line up the digits vertically so that the decimal points line up. Then add or subtract the columns from right to left, carrying or borrowing numbers as necessary.

> **Example:** Add the following numbers: 3.1415 and 2.96.

Step 1: Line up the digits vertically so that the decimal points line up.

$$\begin{array}{r} 3.1415 \\ + \ 2.96 \\ \hline \end{array}$$

Step 2: Add the columns from right to left, carrying when necessary.

$$\begin{array}{r} 1\ 1 \\ 3.1415 \\ + \ 2.96 \\ \hline 6.1015 \end{array}$$

The sum is **6.1015.**

Fractions

Numbers tell you how many; **fractions** tell you *how much of a whole.*

> **Example:** Your class has 24 plants. Your teacher instructs you to put 5 in a shady spot. What fraction does this represent?

Step 1: Write a fraction with the total number of parts in the whole as the denominator.

$$\frac{?}{24}$$

Step 2: Write the number of parts of the whole being represented as the numerator.

$$\frac{5}{24}$$

$\frac{5}{24}$ of the plants will be in the shade.

Reducing Fractions

It is usually best to express a fraction in simplest form. This is called *reducing* a fraction.

> **Example:** Reduce the fraction $\frac{30}{45}$ to its simplest form.

Step 1: Find the largest whole number that will divide evenly into both the numerator and denominator. This number is called the greatest common factor (GCF).

factors of the numerator 30: 1, 2, 3, 5, 6, 10, **15,** 30

factors of the denominator 45: 1, 3, 5, 9, **15,** 45

Step 2: Divide both the numerator and the denominator by the GCF, which in this case is 15.

$$\frac{30}{45} = \frac{30 \div 15}{45 \div 15} = \frac{2}{3}$$

$\frac{30}{45}$ reduced to its simplest form is $\frac{2}{3}$.

Adding and Subtracting Fractions

To **add** or **subtract fractions** that have the **same denominator,** simply add or subtract the numerators.

> **Examples:**
>
> $\frac{3}{5} + \frac{1}{5} = ?$ and $\frac{3}{4} - \frac{1}{4} = ?$

Step 1: Add or subtract the numerators.

$$\frac{3}{5} + \frac{1}{5} = \frac{4}{\quad} \text{ and } \frac{3}{4} - \frac{1}{4} = \frac{2}{\quad}$$

Step 2: Write the sum or difference over the denominator.

$$\frac{3}{5} + \frac{1}{5} = \frac{4}{5} \text{ and } \frac{3}{4} - \frac{1}{4} = \frac{2}{4}$$

Step 3: If necessary, reduce the fraction to its simplest form.

$$\frac{4}{5} \text{ cannot be reduced, and } \frac{2}{4} = \frac{1}{2}.$$

To **add** or **subtract fractions** that have **different denominators,** first find the least common denominator (LCD).

> **Examples:**
>
> $\frac{1}{2} + \frac{1}{6} = ?$ and $\frac{3}{4} - \frac{2}{3} = ?$

Step 1: Write the equivalent fractions with a common denominator.

$$\frac{3}{6} + \frac{1}{6} = ? \text{ and } \frac{9}{12} - \frac{8}{12} = ?$$

Step 2: Add or subtract.

$$\frac{3}{6} + \frac{1}{6} = \frac{4}{6} \text{ and } \frac{9}{12} - \frac{8}{12} = \frac{1}{12}$$

Step 3: If necessary, reduce the fraction to its simplest form.

$$\frac{4}{6} = \frac{2}{3}, \text{ and } \frac{1}{12} \text{ cannot be reduced.}$$

Multiplying Fractions

To **multiply fractions,** multiply the numerators and the denominators together, and then reduce the fraction to its simplest form.

> **Example:**
>
> $\frac{5}{9} \times \frac{7}{10} = ?$

Step 1: Multiply the numerators and denominators.

$$\frac{5}{9} \times \frac{7}{10} = \frac{5 \times 7}{9 \times 10} = \frac{35}{90}$$

Step 2: Reduce.

$$\frac{35}{90} = \frac{35 \div 5}{90 \div 5} = \frac{7}{18}$$

Dividing Fractions

To **divide fractions,** first rewrite the divisor (the number you divide *by*) upside down. This is called the reciprocal of the divisor. Then you can multiply and reduce if necessary.

> **Example:**
>
> $\frac{5}{8} \div \frac{3}{2} = ?$

Step 1: Rewrite the divisor as its reciprocal.

$$\frac{3}{2} \longrightarrow \frac{2}{3}$$

Step 2: Multiply.

$$\frac{5}{8} \times \frac{2}{3} = \frac{5 \times 2}{8 \times 3} = \frac{10}{24}$$

Step 3: Reduce.

$$\frac{10}{24} = \frac{10 \div 2}{24 \div 2} = \frac{5}{12}$$

Scientific Notation

Scientific notation is a short way of representing very large and very small numbers without writing all of the place-holding zeros.

Example: Write 653,000,000 in scientific notation.

Step 1: Write the number without the place-holding zeros.

653

Step 2: Place the decimal point after the first digit.

6.53

Step 3: Find the exponent by counting the number of places that you moved the decimal point.

6.53000000

The decimal point was moved eight places to the left. Therefore, the exponent of 10 is positive 8. Remember, if the decimal point had moved to the right, the exponent would be negative.

Step 4: Write the number in scientific notation.

$$6.53 \times 10^8$$

Area

Area is the number of square units needed to cover the surface of an object.

Formulas:
Area of a square = side × side
Area of a rectangle = length × width
Area of a triangle = $\frac{1}{2}$ × base × height

Examples: Find the areas.

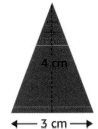

Triangle
Area = $\frac{1}{2}$ × base × height
Area = $\frac{1}{2}$ × 3 cm × 4 cm
Area = **6 cm²**

4 cm

3 cm

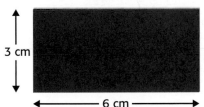

3 cm

6 cm

Rectangle
Area = length × width
Area = 6 cm × 3 cm
Area = **18 cm²**

3 cm

3 cm

Square
Area = side × side
Area = 3 cm × 3 cm
Area = **9 cm²**

Volume

Volume is the amount of space something occupies.

Formulas:
Volume of a cube = side × side × side

Volume of a prism = area of base × height

Examples:
Find the volume of the solids.

Cube
Volume = side × side × side
Volume = 4 cm × 4 cm × 4 cm
Volume = **64 cm³**

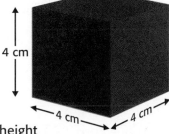

4 cm

4 cm

4 cm

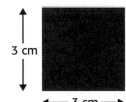

4 cm

3 cm

5 cm

Prism
Volume = area of base × height
Volume = (area of triangle) × height
Volume = $\left(\frac{1}{2} \times 3 \text{ cm} \times 4 \text{ cm} \right) \times 5$ cm
Volume = 6 cm² × 5 cm
Volume = **30 cm³**

Physical Laws and Equations

Law of Conservation of Energy

> The law of conservation of energy states that energy can be neither created nor destroyed.

The total amount of energy in a closed system is always the same. Energy can be changed from one form to another, but all the different forms of energy in a system always add up to the same total amount of energy, no matter how many energy conversions occur.

Law of Universal Gravitation

> The law of universal gravitation states that all objects in the universe attract each other by a force called gravity. The size of the force depends on the masses of the objects and the distance between them.

The first part of the law explains why a bowling ball is much harder to lift than a table-tennis ball. Because the bowling ball has a much larger mass than the table-tennis ball, the amount of gravity between the Earth and the bowling ball is greater than the amount of gravity between the Earth and the table-tennis ball.

The second part of the law explains why a satellite can remain in orbit around the Earth. The satellite is carefully placed at a distance great enough to prevent the Earth's gravity from immediately pulling it down but small enough to prevent it from completely escaping the Earth's gravity and wandering off into space.

Newton's Laws of Motion

> Newton's first law of motion states that an object at rest remains at rest and an object in motion remains in motion at constant speed and in a straight line unless acted on by an unbalanced force.

The first part of the law explains why a football will remain on a tee until it is kicked off or until a gust of wind blows it off.

The second part of the law explains why a bike's rider will continue moving forward after the bike tire runs into a crack in the sidewalk and the bike comes to an abrupt stop until gravity and the sidewalk stop the rider.

> Newton's second law of motion states that the acceleration of an object depends on the mass of the object and the amount of force applied.

The first part of the law explains why the acceleration of a 4 kg bowling ball will be greater than the acceleration of a 6 kg bowling ball if the same force is applied to both.

The second part of the law explains why the acceleration of a bowling ball will be larger if a larger force is applied to it.

The relationship of acceleration (a) to mass (m) and force (F) can be expressed mathematically by the following equation:

$$\text{acceleration} = \frac{force}{mass} \quad \text{or} \quad a = \frac{F}{m}$$

This equation is often rearranged to the form:

$$\text{force} = \text{mass} \times \text{acceleration}$$
$$\text{or}$$
$$F = m \times a$$

> Newton's third law of motion states that whenever one object exerts a force on a second object, the second object exerts an equal and opposite force on the first.

This law explains that a runner is able to move forward because of the equal and opposite force the ground exerts on the runner's foot after each step.

Useful Equations

Average speed

$$\text{Average speed} = \frac{\text{total distance}}{\text{total time}}$$

Example: A bicycle messenger traveled a distance of 136 km in 8 hours. What was the messenger's average speed?

$$\frac{136 \text{ km}}{8 \text{ h}} = 17 \text{ km/h}$$

The messenger's average speed was **17 km/h.**

Average acceleration

$$\text{Average acceleration} = \frac{\text{final velocity} - \text{starting velocity}}{\text{time it takes to change velocity}}$$

Example: Calculate the average acceleration of an Olympic 100 m dash sprinter who reaches a velocity of 15 m/s south at the finish line. The race was in a straight line and lasted 10 s.

$$\frac{15 \text{ m/s} - 0 \text{ m/s}}{10 \text{ s}} = 1.5 \text{ m/s/s}$$

The sprinter's average acceleration is **1.5 m/s/s south.**

Net force

Forces in the Same Direction
When forces are in the same direction, add the forces together to determine the net force.

Example: Calculate the net force on a stalled car that is being pushed by two people. One person is pushing with a force of 13 N northwest and the other person is pushing with a force of 8 N in the same direction.

$$13 \text{ N} + 8 \text{ N} = 21 \text{ N}$$

The net force is **21 N northwest.**

Forces in Opposite Directions
When forces are in opposite directions, subtract the smaller force from the larger force to determine the net force.

Net force (cont'd)

Example: Calculate the net force on a rope that is being pulled on each end. One person is pulling on one end of the rope with a force of 12 N south. Another person is pulling on the opposite end of the rope with a force of 7 N north.

$$12 \text{ N} - 7 \text{ N} = 5 \text{ N}$$

The net force is **5 N south.**

Density

$$\text{Density} = \frac{\text{mass}}{\text{volume}}$$

Example: Calculate the density of a sponge with a mass of 10 g and a volume of 40 mL.

$$\frac{10 \text{ g}}{40 \text{ mL}} = 0.25 \text{ g/mL}$$

The density of the sponge is **0.25 g/mL.**

Pressure

Pressure is the force exerted over a given area. The SI unit for pressure is the pascal, which is abbreviated Pa.

$$\text{Pressure} = \frac{\text{force}}{\text{area}}$$

Example: Calculate the pressure of the air in a soccer ball if the air exerts a force of 10 N over an area of 0.5 m².

$$\text{Pressure} = \frac{10 \text{ N}}{0.5 \text{ m}^2} = 20 \text{ N/m}^2 = 20 \text{ Pa}$$

The pressure of the air inside of the soccer ball is **20 Pa.**

Concentration

$$\text{Concentration} = \frac{\text{mass of solute}}{\text{volume of solvent}}$$

Example: Calculate the concentration of a solution in which 10 g of sugar is dissolved in 125 mL of water.

$$\frac{10 \text{ g of sugar}}{125 \text{ mL of water}} = 0.08 \text{ g/mL}$$

The concentration of this solution is **0.08 g/mL.**

Glossary

A

acid precipitation precipitation that contains acids due to air pollution (23)

air mass a large body of air that has similar temperature and moisture throughout (44)

air pressure the measure of the force with which air molecules push on a surface (5)

altitude the height of an object above the Earth's surface (5)

anemometer (AN uh MAHM uht uhr) a device used to measure wind speed (55)

atmosphere a mixture of gases that surrounds a planet, such as Earth (4)

B

barometer an instrument used to measure air pressure (55)

biome a large region characterized by a specific type of climate and the plants and animals that live there (74)

C

cirrus (SIR uhs) **clouds** thin, feathery white clouds found at high altitudes (41)

climate the average weather conditions in an area over a long period of time (68)

cloud a collection of millions of tiny water droplets or ice crystals (40)

condensation the change of state from a gas to a liquid (39)

conduction the transfer of thermal energy from one material to another by direct contact; conduction can also occur within a substance (11)

convection the transfer of thermal energy by the circulation or movement of a liquid or a gas (11)

Coriolis (KOHR ee OH lis) **effect** the curving of moving objects from a straight path due to the Earth's rotation (15)

cumulus (KYOO myoo luhs) **clouds** puffy, white clouds that tend to have flat bottoms (40)

D

deciduous (dee SIJ oo uhs) describes trees that lose their leaves when the weather becomes cold (78)

density the amount of matter in a given space; mass per unit volume (127)

dew point the temperature to which air must cool to be completely saturated (39)

E

elevation the height of an object above sea level; the height of surface landforms above sea level (72)

El Niño periodic change in the location of warm and cool surface waters in the Pacific Ocean (94)

evaporation the change of state from a liquid to a vapor (36)

evergreens trees that keep their leaves year-round (78)

F

front the boundary that forms between two different air masses (46)

G

glacier an enormous mass of moving ice (83)

global warming a rise in average global temperatures (12, 86)

greenhouse effect the natural heating process of a planet, such as the Earth, by which gases in the atmosphere trap thermal energy (12, 86)

H

humidity the amount of water vapor or moisture in the air (37)

hurricane a large, rotating tropical weather system with wind speeds of at least 119 km/h (51)

hypothesis a possible explanation or answer to a question (116)

I

ice age a period during which ice collects in high latitudes and moves toward lower latitudes (83)

isobars lines that connect points of equal air pressure (57)

J

jet streams narrow belts of high-speed winds that blow in the upper troposphere and the lower stratosphere (18)

L

latitude the distance north or south from the equator; measured in degrees (69)

lightning the large electrical discharge that occurs between two oppositely charged surfaces (49)

M

mass the amount of matter that something is made of; its value does not change with the object's location (113)

mesosphere the coldest layer of the atmosphere (8)

meteorology the study of the entire atmosphere (64)

microclimate a small region with unique climatic characteristics (82)

O

observation any use of the senses to gather information (116)

ozone a gas molecule that is made up of three oxygen atoms and that absorbs ultraviolet radiation from the sun (7)

P

polar easterlies wind belts that extend from the poles to 60° latitude in both hemispheres (17)

polar zone the northernmost and southernmost climate zones (80)

precipitation solid or liquid water that falls from the air to the Earth (36, 42)

prevailing winds winds that blow mainly from one direction (71)

primary pollutants pollutants that are put directly into the air by human or natural activity (21)

psychrometer (sie KRAHM uht uhr) an instrument used to measure relative humidity (38)

R

radiation the transfer of energy as electromagnetic waves, such as visible light or infrared waves (10)

relative humidity the amount of moisture the air contains compared with the maximum amount it can hold at a particular temperature (37)

S

scientific method a series of steps that scientists use to answer questions and solve problems (116)

secondary pollutants pollutants that form from chemical reactions that occur when primary pollutants come in contact with other primary pollutants or with naturally occurring substances, such as water vapor (21)

smog a photochemical fog produced by the reaction of sunlight and air pollutants (21)

solar energy energy from the sun (10)

station model a small circle showing the location of a weather station along with a set of symbols and numbers surrounding it that represent weather data (56)

storm surge a local rise in sea level near the shore that is caused by strong winds from a storm, such as a hurricane (53)

stratosphere the atmospheric layer above the troposphere (7)

stratus (STRAT uhs) **clouds** clouds that form in layers (40)

surface current a streamlike movement of water that occurs at or near the surface of the ocean (73)

T

temperate zone the climate zone between the Tropics and the polar zone (78)

temperature a measure of how hot (or cold) something is (8, 54)

thermometer a tool used to measure air temperature (54)

thermosphere the uppermost layer of the atmosphere (8)

thunder the sound that results from the rapid expansion of air along a lightning strike (49)

thunderstorms small, intense weather systems that produce strong winds, heavy rain, lightning, and thunder (48)

tornado a small, rotating column of air that has high wind speeds and low central pressure and that touches the ground (50)

trade winds the winds that blow from 30° latitude to the equator (16)

tropical zone the warm zone located around the equator (75)

troposphere (TROH poh SFIR) the lowest layer of the atmosphere (7)

V

volume the amount of space that something occupies or the amount of space that something contains (125)

W

water cycle the continuous movement of water from water sources into the air, onto land, into and over the ground, and back to the water sources; a cycle that links all of the Earth's solid, liquid, and gaseous water together (36)

weather the condition of the atmosphere at a particular time and place (36, 68)

weather forecast a prediction of future weather conditions over the next 3 to 5 days (54)

westerlies wind belts found in both the Northern and Southern Hemispheres between 30° and 60° latitude (17)

wind moving air (14)

wind energy energy in wind (17)

windsock a device used to measure wind direction (55)

wind vane a device used to measure wind direction (55)

Index

A **boldface** number refers to an illustration on that page.

A

acceleration, average, 127
acid precipitation, 23, **23**
air, 20, **71**. *See also* air pollution; atmosphere
air masses, **44**, 44–47, **47**
air pollution
    car exhaust and, **21**, 22, 87
    cure for, 33
    health effects of, 24, **24**
    indoor, 22
    particulates in, 32
    remediation of, 24–25, 33
    sources of, 22
    types of, 21, **21**
air pressure, 5, **5, 6, 14,** 14–19, **57**
air temperature, 6, **6**
altitude, 5
anemometers, 55, **55**
area
    calculation of, 125
    defined, 125
atmosphere, 25. *See also* air; weather
    composition, 4–5
    heating of, 10–13
    layers of, **6,** 6–9
    pollution of, 20–25, 33. *See also* air pollution
    pressure and temperature, **5,** 5–6, **6, 14,** 14–15, 54
    water vapor in, 7, 36–40, 42
    weather and, 55–56
auroras, 9, **9**
averages, defined, 122

B

barometers, 55
biomes, 74–82, **74–82**
Bradbury, Ray, 65
breezes, **18,** 18–19, **19**
bubonic plague, 94

C

carbon dioxide
    greenhouse effect and, 12, **12,** 86–87
careers in science
    meteorologist, 64, 95
cars
    electric, 33, **33**
    pollution from, 21, **21,** 25, **25**

Celsius scale, 114
chaparrals, **74, 78,** 79, **79**
Clean Air Act of 1970, 24
climate, 68–87. *See also* weather
    changes in, 83–87, 95
    elevation and, 72
    global warming, 12–13, 86–87
    ice ages and, **83,** 83–85
    latitude and, 69, **69**
    microclimates, 82
    models, 95
    mountains and, 72, **72**
    prevailing winds, 71, **71, 72**
    surface currents and, 73, **73**
    volcanoes and, 85, **85**
    zones, 74, **74,** 75, 78, 80
clouds, **40,** 40–42, **41**
    formation of, 40–41
    funnel clouds, 50, **50**
    height of, **41**
    types of, 40–41, **40–41**
cold air masses, 45, **46**
cold fronts, **46, 57**
concentration, calculation of, 127
concept mapping, 112
condensation, **36, 39,** 39–40
conduction, 11, **11**
conifers, 82
conservation of energy, law of, 126
continental drift, 85
continental polar (cP) air masses, **44**
continental tropical (cT) air masses, **44**
controlled experiments, 117
convection
    in the atmosphere, 11, **11**
convection cells, 15, **15**
convection currents, 11, **11**
conversion tables, SI, 113
Coriolis effect, 15, **15**
currents
    climate and, 73, **73**
    convection, 11, **11**
cyclones, 51. *See also* hurricanes

D

deciduous trees, 78
decimals, 123
deforestation, 87, **87**
density
    of air, **71**
    calculation of, 127
deserts
    temperate, **74, 78,** 80, **80**
    tropical, **74, 75,** 76, **76**
dew point, 39
dinosaurs, 32
doldrums, 17

Doppler radar, 56, **56**
dry-bulb thermometer, 38

E

Earth. *See also* atmosphere; maps; plate tectonics
    latitude, **69,** 69–70, **70**
    orbital changes and climate, 84, **84**
electric cars, 33, **33**
electricity
    for cars, 25, 33, **33**
    from wind energy, 17, **17**
elevation, 72
El Niño, 94
energy
    in the atmosphere, 10–11
    transfer of, 10–11, **10–11**
    wind, 17, **17**
Environmental Protection Agency (EPA), 24–25
evaporation, **36**
evergreens, 78
experiments, controlled, 117

F

Fahrenheit–Celsius conversion, 114
Fahrenheit scale, 114, **114**
fingernail growth, 13
first law of motion (Newton's), 126
fog, 40
force(s)
    calculation of, 127
forests, temperate, **74,** 78, **78**
fossil fuels,
    problems with, 23–24
fractions, 123–124
fronts, 46–47, **46–47, 57**
funnel clouds, 50, **50**

G

gases
    greenhouse, 12
geography, 72, **72**
glacial periods, 83, **83**
glaciers
    continental drift and, 85
    interglacial periods, 83–84
glaze ice, 42, **42**

global warming, 12–13, 86–87. *See also* climate
global winds, **16,** 16–18
graduated cylinder, 115, **115**

Credits

Abbreviations used: (t) top, (c) center, (b) bottom, (l) left, (r) right, (bkgd) background

ILLUSTRATIONS

All work, unless otherwise noted, contributed by Holt, Rinehart & Winston.

Table of Contents: Page vi, Stephen Durke/Washington Artists, vii(globe), Uhl Studios, Inc.; vii(arrows), Stephen Durke/Washington Artists.

Chapter One: Page 4(b), Sidney Jablonski; 5(br), Stephen Durke/Washington Artists; 6(b), Stephen Durke/Washington Artists; 7(c), Stephen Durke/Washington Artists; 8, Stephen Durke/Washington Artists; 10(b), Uhl Studios, Inc.; 11(b), Uhl Studios, Inc.; 12(c), John Huxtable/Black Creative; 14(bl), Uhl Studios, Inc.; 14(bl), Stephen Durke/Washington Artists; 15(tr), Uhl Studios, Inc.; 15(br), Stephen Durke/Washington Artists; 16(b), Uhl Studios, Inc.; 16(b), Stephen Durke/Washington Artists; 18, Stephen Durke/Washington Artists; 19, Stephen Durke/Washington Artists; 21(b), John Huxtable/Black Creative; 29(c), Stephen Durke/Washington Artists.

Chapter Two: Page 36(b), Robert Hynes; 41(b), Stephen Durke/Washington Artists; 42(tl), Stephen Durke/Washington Artists; 44(b), MapQuest.com; 46, Stephen Durke/Washington Artists; 47, Stephen Durke/Washington Artists; 49(br), Paul DiMare; 52(b), Paul DiMare; 54(tr), Dan McGeehan/Koralick Associates; 57(cr), MapQuest.com; 63(cr), MapQuest.com.

Chapter Three: Page 69(br), Uhl Studios, Inc.; 69(br), Stephen Durke/Washington Artists; 70(c), Craig Attebery/Jeff Lavaty Artist Agent; 71(tc), Stephen Durke/Washington Artists; 72(b), Uhl Studios, Inc.; 73(c), MapQuest.com; 74(cl), Stephen Durke/Washington Artists; 74(b), MapQuest.com; 75(tr), Stephen Durke/Washington Artists; 75(c), MapQuest.com; 78(tl), Stephen Durke/Washington Artists; 78(c), MapQuest.com; 80(bl), Stephen Durke/Washington Artists; 81(t), MapQuest.com; 83(bl), MapQuest.com; 83(tr), Marty Roper/Planet Rep; 84, Sidney Jablonski; 85(c), Uhl Studios, Inc.; 85(br), MapQuest.com; 86(b), Marty Roper/Planet Rep; 90(t), Craig Attebery/Jeff Lavaty Artist Agent; 90(cr), Stephen Durke/Washington Artists; 92(tr), Terry Kovalcik; 93(cr), Sidney Jablonski.

LabBook: Page 103(tr), Mark Heine; 106(t), MapQuest.com.

Appendix: Page 114(c), Terry Guyer; 118(b), Mark Mille/Sharon Langley.

PHOTOGRAPHY

Cover and Title Page: William Lesch/The Image Bank

Sam Dudgeon/HRW Photo: Page viii-1, 7(bc), 24, 33(t), 37, 38, 43(cr), 54, 96, 97(bc), 98(br,cl), 99(tl,b), 101, 102, 110, 115(br).

Table of Contents: Page v(t), Tom Bean; v(b), Sam Dudgeon/HRW Photo; vi(t), NASA/Science Photo Library/Photo Researchers, Inc.; vi(b), Eric Sandler/Liaison Agency; vii(c), Roger Werth/Woodfin Camp & Associates; vii(b), NASA.

Chapter One: Pages 2-3 Joseph McBride/Stone; p. 3 HRW Photo; p. 5, Peter Van Steen/HRW Photo; p. 7(tr), SuperStock; p. 8(b), Image Copyright ©(2001) PhotoDisc, Inc.; p. 9, Johnny Johnson/DRK Photo; p. 13, Renee Lynn/Photo Researchers, Inc.; p. 14(tr), Jaime Puebla/AP/Wide World Photos; p. 17(tr), A&L Sinibaldi/Stone; p. 17(cl), Luc Marescot/Liaison Agency; p. 18(tl), NASA/Science Photo Library/Photo Researchers, Inc.; p. 20, Byron Augustin/Tom Stack & Associates; p. 21(tc), Argus Potoarchiv/Peter Arnold, Inc.; p. 21(cr), Bruce Forster/Stone; p. 21(tr), David Weintraub/Photo Researchers, Inc; p. 22(tl), Robert Ginn/PhotoEdit; p. 22(cr), Phil Schofield/Picture Quest; p. 23(cl), Jean Lauzon/Publiphoto/Photo Researchers, Inc.; p. 23(cr), David Woodfall/Stone; p. 23(br), NASA; p. 25(tl), SuperStock; p. 25(tr), Chromosohm/Sohm/Photo Researchers, Inc.; p. 27 Sam Dudgeon/HRW Photo; p. 30(bl), Telegraph Colour Library/FPG International; p. 30(tr), Salaber/Liaison Agency; p. 32(c), Bill Thompson/Woodfin Camp & Associates, Inc.; p. 33(tr), Steve Winter/Black Star.

Chapter Two: pp. 34-35 Merrilee Thomas/Tom Stack & Associates; 35 HRW Photo; p. 39, Victoria Smith/HRW Photo; p. 40(cl), Eric Sandler/Liaison Agency; p. 40(bl), NOAA; p. 41(tr), Joyce Photographics/Photo Researchers, Inc.; p. 42(cl), Muridsany et Perennou/Science Source/Photo Researchers, Inc.; p. 42(br), Jim Mone/AP/Wide World Photos; p. 43(tr), Gene E. Moore; p. 45(br), Image Copyright ©2001 PhotoDisc, Inc.; p. 45(tr), Rod Planck/Tom Stack & Associates; p. 48, Kent Wood/Peter Arnold, Inc.; p. 49(br), Jean-Loup Charmet/Science Photo Library/Photo Researchers, Inc.; p. 50(all), Howard B. Bluestein/Photo Researchers, Inc.; p. 51(tr), Red Huber/Orlando Sentinel/SYGMA; p. 51(bl), NASA; p. 52(tl), NASA/Science Photo Library/Photo Researchers, Inc.; p. 53, Victor R. Caivano/AP/Wide World Photos; p. 55(cl), David Hwang/Mazer Corp.; p. 55(br), G.R. Roberts Photo Library; p. 56(tl), Tom Bean; p. 56(cr), David R. Frazier/Photolibrary; p. 59 Sam Dudgeon/HRW Photo; pp. 60-61, The American Map Corporation/ADC The Map People; p. 62(tr), Clyde H. Smith/Peter Arnold, Inc.; p. 63, Jean-Loup Charmet/Science Photo Library/Photo Researchers, Inc.; p. 64(br), Salaber/Liaison Agency; p. 64(tl), Michael Lyon.

Chapter Three: pp. 66-67 Karen Dickey; p. 66 Steve Bloom Images; p. 67 HRW Photo; p. 68(bkgd), Tom Van Sant, Geosphere Project/Planetary Visions/Science Photo Library/Photo Researchers, Inc.; p. 68(tl), G.R. Roberts Photo Library; p. 68(tr), Index Stock; p. 68(c), Yva Momatiuk & John Eastcott; p. 68(bl), Gary Retherford/Photo Researchers, Inc.; p. 68(br), Thomas Van Sant, Geosphere Project/Planetary Visions/Science Photo Library/Photo Researchers, Inc.; p. 69(tc), Michael Newman/Photo Edit; p. 69(tr), Kim Heacox/DRK Photo; p. 71(b), Tom Van Sant, Geosphere Project/Planetary Visions/Science Photo Library/Photo Researchers, Inc.; p. 72(bl), Larry Ulrich Photography; p. 72(br), Paul Wakefield/Stone; p. 75(bc), Michael Fogden/Bruce Coleman, Inc.; p. 76(l), Thomas A. Wiewandt; p. 76(c), Larry Ulrich Photography; p. 77, Nadine Zuber/Photo Researchers, Inc.; p. 78, Carr Clifton/Minden Pictures; p. 79(tl), Tom Bean/Stone; p. 79(bc), Fred Hirschmann; p. 80(c), Steven Simpson/FPG International; p. 81, Harry Walker/Alaska Stock; p. 82, SuperStock; p. 85(tr), Roger Werth/Woodfin Camp & Associates; p. 87(tr), Jacques Jangoux/Tony Stone Images; p. 87(cr), Leverett Bradley/Stone; p. 91, Danilo G. Donadoni/Bruce Coleman Inc.; p. 92(bl), Richard Pharoah/International Stock; p. 94, George Bernard/Animals Animals/Earth Scenes; p. 95, Hank Morgan/Photo Researchers, Inc. .

LabBook/Appendix: "LabBook Header", "L", Corbis Images; "a", Letraset Phototone; "b", and "B", HRW; "o", and "k", images ©2001 PhotoDisc/HRW; Page 97(tr), John Langford/HRW Photo; 97(cl), Michelle Bridwell/HRW Photo; 97(br), Image ©2001 PhotoDisc, Inc./HRW; 98(bl), Stephanie Morris/HRW Photo; 99(b), Peter Van Steen/HRW Photo; 99(tr), Jana Birchum/HRW Photo; 105, Kuni Stringer/AP/Wide World Photos; 106, Victoria Smith/HRW Photo; 107, Jay Malonson/AP/Wide World Photos; 111, Andy Christiansen/HRW Photo; 115(tr), Peter Van Steen/HRW Photo.

Feature Borders: Unless otherwise noted below, all images ©2001 PhotoDisc/HRW. "Across the Sciences" 94, all images by HRW; "Careers" sand bkgd and Saturn, Corbis Images; DNA, Morgan Cain & Associates; scuba gear, ©1997 Radlund & Associates for Artville; "Health Watch" 32, dumbbell, Sam Dudgeon/HRW Photo; aloe vera, EKG, Victoria Smith/HRW Photo; basketball, ©1997 Radlund & Associates for Artville; shoes, bubbles, Greg Geisler; "Scientific Debate" 33, Sam Dudgeon/HRW Photo; "Science Fiction" 65, saucers, Ian Christopher/Greg Geisler; book, HRW; bkgd, Stock Illustration Source; "Science Technology and Society" 95.

Self-Check Answers

Chapter 1—The Atmosphere

Page 6: As you climb a mountain, the air becomes less dense because there are fewer air molecules. So even though cold air is generally more dense than warm air, it is less dense at higher elevations.

Chapter 2—Understanding Weather

Page 38: Evaporation occurs when liquid water changes into water vapor and returns to the air. Humidity is the amount of water vapor in the air.

Chapter 3—Climate

Page 70: Australia has summer during our winter months, December–February.

Page 76: Because of its dryness, desert soil is poor in organic matter, which fertilizes the soil. Without this natural fertilizer, crops would not be able to grow.

Page 84: The Earth's elliptical orbit causes seasonal differences. When the Earth's orbit is more elliptical, summers are hotter because the Earth is closer to the sun and receives more solar radiation. Winters are cooler because the Earth is farther from the sun and receives less solar radiation.